CW00548491

PRAISE FOR

## The Gig Mindset Advantage

"In her provocative new book, Jane McConnell's deeply researched exploration of the origins, evolution, and implications of the gig mindset offers leaders and managers actionable insights into the realities of today's and tomorrow's workplaces."
**Jon Husband, founder of Wirearchy**

"At once a manifesto and an action plan that details how a range of humane and inclusive behaviors, traits, and principles can re-make diverse teams and businesses into more resilient, innovative, and purposeful organizations."
**David Slocum, academic director at Rare with Google**

"Will inspire individuals to lead no matter what their title, and help organizations create a more agile, collaborative culture."
**John Stepper, author of *Working Out Loud***

"Challenges us to think about the future of our organizations, and, more importantly, of our people, in a way that transcends cultures and structures."
**Stéphane Aknin, VP of Creative & Content at Prudential Financial, Inc.**

"*The Gig Mindset Advantage* is a compass for business, and Jane McConnell is the scout that every executive should tap to help them find their way to the future of work."
**Chris Shipley, coauthor of *The Adaptation Advantage: Let Go, Learn Fast, and Thrive in the Future of Work***

"A must-read for anyone who wants to stay relevant and for any leader who wants to ensure the future of their organization."
**Frédérique Thiriet-Smith, change and learning expert at BASF**

"Change is afoot in the world of work and the gig mindset is an important harbinger of that change. This book examines it from many angles and offers compelling ways to adapt. A must-read for every talent professional."

"Now more than ever a gig mindset is a requirement for those seeking to make a greater impact within their company, especially during times of change. Whether you are an individual contributor, a team manager, or a CEO, you will be sure to gain new insight and understanding here."

"In the 'future of work' canon, *The Gig Mindset Advantage* is a rare treat."

"Jane McConnell explores how the gig mindset allows us to focus on ourselves, our real needs, and the contribution we want to bring to the world. Her research and stories show how each of us can play a role in building a gig-mindset ecosystem in our organizations and open a new world of opportunities."

# The Gig
# Mindset
# Advantage

Martin –

Thank you for your support over many years –

Jane

# The Gig Mindset Advantage

Why a Bold New Breed of
Employee Is Your Organization's
Secret Weapon in Volatile Times

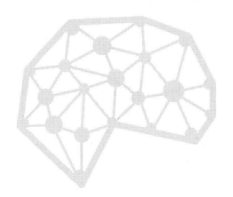

## Jane McConnell

**Figure.1**

*Vancouver / Berkeley*

*Cataloguing data is available from Library and Archives Canada*
ISBN 978-1-77327-150-7 (hbk.)
ISBN 978-1-77327-151-4 (ebook)
ISBN 978-1-77327-152-1 (pdf)

Jacket design by Jessica Sullivan and Naomi MacDougall
Interior design by Naomi MacDougall
Front jacket images: agsandrew/Shutterstock.com;
karpechenkov/Shutterstock.com

Editing by Tyee Bridge
Copy editing by Judy Phillips
Proofreading by Alison Strobel
Indexing by Stephen Ullstrom

Printed and bound in Canada by Friesens
Distributed internationally by Publishers Group West

Figure 1 Publishing Inc.
Vancouver BC Canada
www.figure1publishing.com

To Russ Collins, whose practical and moral support
made this book possible.

# Contents

THE WHY

THE HOW

THE HOW

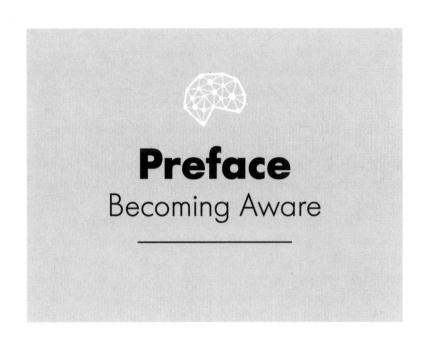

# Preface
## Becoming Aware

**In 2018, I keynoted** a conference about the advantages a gig mindset brings to organizations. A senior communications director of a global insurance group came up to me the minute I finished and asked, "How can we bring this mindset inside our company?" He was the first person at a high management level to ask me that question. He saw the value of the gig mindset but had no idea how to cultivate it in his company.

Attempting to answer it is why I wrote this book—and my interest in it is personal as well as professional.

I've been a gig worker for over 20 years, working primarily with organizations in Europe and North America as a strategic adviser for their internal digital strategies. This has brought me firsthand experience with over one hundred organizations and many hundreds of managers in different sectors and countries. There were always a few people who stood out from the others. People who dared to do things differently because they believed there was a better way. I saw what I perceived to be *freelancer-type* behavior in these people. Although they were full-time, salaried employees, their behavior seemed counter to the way most people work. They were at ease taking initiatives without prior management approval, uncommon behavior in most organizations. I saw a few who went so far as to get people together to tackle a problem without their supervisor even knowing there was an issue to be solved. Now and then, the issue crossed organizational silos, but these people ignored the traditional protocol of starting with a manager-to-manager agreement and just jumped in, spontaneously working together on the challenge.

After talking with these people and watching how they worked, interacted with colleagues and management, and, especially, how they related to me—eager to see my perspective as an outsider—I decided I needed to better understand them, their challenges and motivations. There were not many people like this, and as I observed more closely, I saw that this so-called freelancer behavior took place in specific contexts. It occurred in individual people, rarely in teams; usually went unnoticed by others; and was dependent on the specific person. If that person disappeared, so did the behavior. Very often I sensed underlying emotions, ranging from extreme frustration to extreme pride.

As a lifelong freelancer, I felt a strong affinity for what I was seeing in these people. I have always been a true gig worker, self-employed and working from client project to client project. But these people were acting like I did even though they were in an organizational context. I was seeing gig workers inside corporations, government agencies, educational institutions, not-for-profit groups and international organizations—and all with full-time, salaried jobs. This deserved a deeper investigation.

I coined a phrase for this phenomenon—*the gig-mindset inside*—and decided to investigate the advantages and disadvantages it brings to people and to organizations. The more I explored, the more obvious it became that it was primarily an advantage, and so I began to think in terms of the *gig-mindset advantage*. Although still rare, from what I could see, if confirmed by research, this new phenomenon would be a fundamental shift in how people see work and how organizations function. When you look at how the workplace has evolved over the past 20 years (see Appendix B1), you can see why the gig mindset was destined to emerge—as well as why it is happening so slowly.

## Discovering the gig mindset

In 2018, I put together an advisory board of 16 people from 10 countries who worked in diverse industries to help me shape an international survey of the gig mindset. We decided to define it in terms of apparent opposites—the traditional mindset versus the gig mindset. Together, with much discussion back and forth, we defined eight qualities or behaviors at each end of the spectrum, did test runs, then launched the survey. The survey also included questions about organizational and work cultures. The full set of questions is shared in Appendix A5.

We then conducted a survey of just under three hundred people from Asia, Europe, and North America. Members of the advisory board helped me with the data analysis and findings that you will discover throughout this book. Following the data analysis, I conducted 31 hour-long interviews with people around the world in order to get deeper, qualitative, personal stories.[1]

While the survey was taking place, I consulted research papers and books from past years about organizational and management strategies, and talked with experts who had studied these subjects in depth. I found myself drawn to the topics of building resilience, improvisation, and new ways of learning. The gig-mindset behaviors, which I discuss later, are tightly coupled with these topics.

The gig-mindset research took place after 10 years of studies I had conducted from 2006 through 2016 in the form of yearly surveys, exploring the state of the organization in the digital age. This had resulted in 10 annual reports drawing on data from three hundred to four hundred organizations annually. They were from private and public sectors, with workforces ranging from under a thousand to over a hundred thousand, operating in a wide range of industries, including banking, healthcare, manufacturing, construction, and more.[2] The data and stories gathered over time show the slow emergence of what today I am calling the gig mindset. The emergence of the gig mindset is an important milestone in a long, continual transformation of people and the workplace.

## A new identity

I mention earlier that I keynoted a conference in 2018, where I talked about the advantages of the gig mindset. In fact, I had that opportunity three times during that year—in Berlin, London, and Paris—each time with very different audiences from very different cultures. Each time I shaped my talk around the gig-mindset advantage inside organizations, and each time I was surprised to find myself surrounded by audience members at the coffee break. They told me how much they appreciated my talk, how I had helped them understand some of the difficulties they were having at work, and how I had validated how they worked. They recognized themselves in my description, and several said they had never realized it had a name—which until then it didn't.

A new way of seeing themselves materialized for many of the people I talked with at those three events in 2018. They were saying things like "Thank you for giving me an identity. I had always felt something was wrong with me!"

Many people shared their frustrations and, in some cases, the serious problems they were having in their organizations because of how management perceived their work. "You're the first person to understand me," said one. "Now I know why I have the problems at work I have," said another.

We will see later how the traditional reaction of management often drives gig-mindset activities underground or off the radar. When they are discovered, they are either ignored or squashed—resulting in indirect punishment or ostracism of the initiators—or applauded and integrated into business practices.

The input and stories shared by research participants brought me to a deeper understanding of what is happening inside many organizations today. This book is an attempt to share what I learned, so that you too may benefit from these learnings and move toward developing a gig-mindset advantage within yourself and your organization.

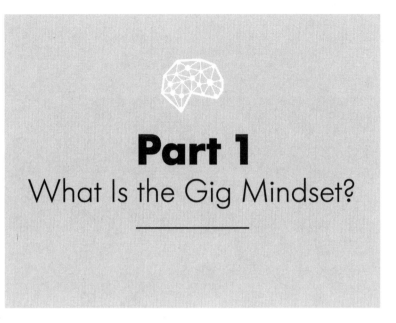

# Part 1
## What Is the Gig Mindset?

**The gig mindset** is a way of working where people take initiatives, experiment with new methods, and share their work openly. Gig mindsetters network extensively, interacting, sharing, and contributing information with others. They keep their eyes on what's happening in the external world. They do not hesitate to question the status quo and often come up with new ways to deal with problems and challenges. These qualities—described inside the circle in the chart below—help manage risk and build proactive resilience for the organization. In this world, leadership is not hierarchical but rather the influence coming from any part of the organization that brings change. The resulting work culture brings benefits to the organization in many ways, as you will discover throughout this book.

However, unless management is aware of the benefits of having a work culture oriented toward the gig mindset, the organization runs a risk of disappearing or diminishing its place in the world. Gig mindsetters are not troublemakers causing problems, even though

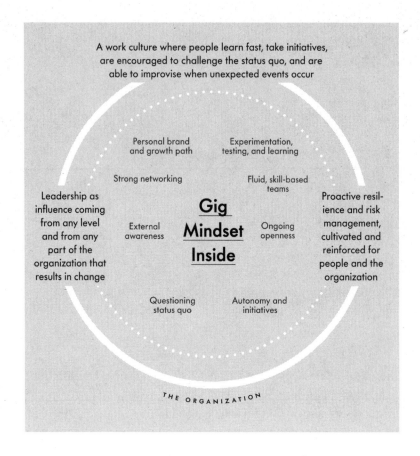

A work culture where people learn fast, take initiatives, are encouraged to challenge the status quo, and are able to improvise when unexpected events occur

Personal brand and growth path

Experimentation, testing, and learning

Strong networking

Fluid, skill-based teams

Leadership as influence coming from any level and from any part of the organization that results in change

External awareness

**Gig Mindset Inside**

Ongoing openness

Proactive resilience and risk management, cultivated and reinforced for people and the organization

Questioning status quo

Autonomy and initiatives

THE ORGANIZATION

some I have talked with have experienced that reaction. In reality, they trigger change and enable organizations to face the future with both ambition and serenity.

A CEO in a mid-size US-based company sees the strategic big picture:

The gig mindset is the real competitive advantage for the future.

A manager in a global transportation company in Scandinavia believes it is a priority to retain people with a gig mindset:

If I, as a manager, don't encourage the gig mindset, I will lose my own motivation and, in the end, the best people.

A senior manager in Switzerland in a UN agency foresees the future:

Today, people with a gig mindset are the exception, not the rule. But it's like they're early adopters who may well become the rule in the future.

These three leaders know the importance of the gig mindset. Most people do not yet understand it. The greatest risk today is to ignore it. The gig mindset tends to be resisted by the organizational immune system because it threatens hierarchy, questions the status quo, and breaks through invisible barriers.

## Why is the gig mindset important?

Gig mindsetters are a new breed of employee who dare to challenge the traditional thinking and ways of working that in the end will make the organization more resilient and successful in volatile times. They are in effect a secret weapon for the organization. However, they are unseen and not yet recognized for their impact. Once they are seen in a new light and understood by management, celebrated and encouraged, they can inspire others, stimulate new thinking, and help the organization build strength and self-sustaining resilience.

### QUESTIONS TO ASK YOURSELF

Take a look at the two sets of questions below—the first for people in general and the second for high-level leaders. Answer the four questions by responding "yes," "sometimes," "rarely," or "no."[1]

**You, the individual**

❶ Are you comfortable questioning the status quo in your organization for work practices or business strategies?

❷ Do you often "work out loud"—making your project work visible to people outside the immediate team before it is finished, and soliciting feedback from others?

❸ When you see a problem, do you feel free to take the initiative of working with others to solve it, without first getting approval from your manager?

❹ Do you spend a significant amount of time on external networking, to learn and share with people outside your organization?

If you answered "yes" or "sometimes" to two or more of the questions, the way you work is likely gig-mindset oriented.

**You, the senior leader**

❶ Are people in your organization able to communicate directly with you or your immediate team when they have ideas that may challenge the status quo, without having to go through layers of management?

❷ Do you encourage teams across your organization to work out loud, sharing their work in an ongoing way before it is completed?

❸ When an experimental initiative fails, do you consider it a positive experience and ask the people involved to share what they learned?

❹ Do you give people time for outside activities such as external networking, attending conferences, and taking external online learning programs?

If you answered "yes" or "sometimes" to two or more of the questions, you are likely one of the rare senior managers cultivating a gig-mindset approach to work in your organization.

## Why does the gig mindset make some people uncomfortable?

The CEO of a company specializing in workplace design for education, healthcare, and retail industries explained why gig mindsetters are perceived to be a threat to most organizations and traditional leaders:

> We are seeing roles and processes being converted into skills required for performance. When you eliminate roles, you start to fracture hierarchy. The culture, the technology, communication, employee performance reviews, and nearly every other aspect of traditional business structure is stressed.

When we compare the eight traits of the gig mindset with the traditional mindset as studied in the research, we can see exactly what the CEO quoted above is talking about.

1. In the gig-mindset culture, experimentation and test-and-learn methods are important, and failure is considered to be a learning opportunity. In the traditional-mindset culture, proven and approved methods are preferred.

2. Gig mindsetters believe roles in projects should be determined by skills, and that different skills are required at different times during the project. People with a traditional mindset prefer a clear definition of roles and responsibilities, established by the manager.

3. Gig mindsetters believe that working openly on projects and making work visible before it is finished is valuable because people outside the team may have information, ideas, or contacts that will enrich the project. Those with a traditional mindset, on the other hand, prefer to wait until the project is finished, to avoid the risk of showing imperfections that could negatively impact the team professionally.

4. Gig mindsetters feel free to take initiatives when they identify issues others have not seen. They act, making decisions and assuming responsibility for the outcome. People with a traditional mindset

prefer decisions to flow down the chain, bringing consistency and control across the organization.

5. Gig mindsetters do not hesitate to question the status quo and express doubt when they believe there is a better way of doing something. They do not hesitate to contradict what is taken for granted by others. A person with a traditional mindset sees no need to question something that has worked so far, because they believe stability and consistency in work and business practices are important.

6. Gig mindsetters believe that trends and developments in the external world—economy, technology, social, culture—are important to follow, as they may directly or indirectly impact the organization. People with a traditional mindset, however, feel it is sufficient to focus primarily on what is happening inside the organization—projects, events, activities, people—rather than spending time watching the external world.

7. Gig mindsetters realize that both internal and external networking are valuable in building relationships, and in learning and sharing with others. People with a traditional mindset interact primarily with internal networks and believe there is little need to participate in external networking.

8. Gig mindsetters see personal advancement as an expansion of expertise, experience, and capabilities rather than as a career move per se. They think in terms of marketable skills that represent the value and contributions they are able to offer. On the other hand, people with a traditional mindset believe they were hired do a job, and acquire more skills and knowledge in order to progress up the corporate ladder.

In short, the gig-mindset approach threatens established ways of working. Although it has been emerging for some time, it is new for many. When people encounter something new, they tend to react in one of three ways: they ignore it, they fight it, or they embrace it. These reactions to the gig mindset by people at different levels and in different functions are no exception.

**Response 1: They ignore it.** If people see no use for the gig mindset, they will ignore it. They simply will not see that something new is happening.

To recognize and cultivate the gig mindset, you must first understand it. So, the first goal of this book is to make clear what the gig mindset is and how it brings new life to organizations, making them more competitive and positioning them to thrive both now and in the future.

**Response 2: They fight it.** If people feel threatened by the gig mindset—for example, if it calls into question how they are accustomed to working or their position in the organization—they will fight it.

A second goal of this book is to explore why there is so much resistance to the gig mindset. Understanding the *why* of resistance will enable you to overcome it. People who work in a gig-mindset way are often perceived by management as inconsistent, unpredictable, and uncontrollable. They project a sense of not having a far-reaching fixed plan, and of improvising and playing things by ear. This makes people who are accustomed to detailed strategies and preapproved action plans uncomfortable.

**Response 3: They embrace it.** If people see how the gig mindset will help their own work and bring value to the organization, they will embrace it.

The third and most important goal of this book is to suggest strategic and practical ways to trigger, grow, and develop the gig mindset in yourself and in your organization.

## A naturally emerging, bottom-up movement

Today, the gig mindset is a bottom-up and individually driven movement. Tomorrow it will become the accepted and encouraged way of working, where leaders will be proud to say they have a gig-mindset work culture.

This is not the first time that bottom-up movements have changed the workplace. Others that started with unofficial, unapproved initiatives and ended up becoming official enterprise solutions include the internal use of social media, BYOD (bring your own device), and cloud storage services. Often, the most active, high-performing people used these solutions out of necessity, doing what they had to do to get their jobs done. Like these earlier movements, the gig mindset is happening spontaneously through interactions and experiments inside organizations, often among employees inventing new ways of working because they feel the old ways are no longer effective.

The new capabilities and interactive flows are the background from which the gig mindset is taking shape. It is opening new ways of thinking, of acting, and of making sense of the work as well as life. Let's summarize:

### WHAT THE GIG MINDSET IS

- A bottom-up movement emerging in organizations around the world

- A new identity for people and organizations

- A framework for thinking, organizing, interacting, and working

- A set of behaviors and attitudes that counter old behaviors that block or slow progress

- A form of risk management; a way to build resilience based on people and behaviors, essential in today's uncertain environment

## A compass, not a map

This book does not outline a method nor a model to be followed. It does not set out detailed strategic steps. Instead, it offers ideas and stories from others from which you can define your own principles and actions. Strategies change with time and circumstances, but principles last longer.

## WHAT THE GIG MINDSET IS NOT

- A method or model for reinventing yourself or your organization

- A top-down or structured change method

- A strategic road map

- A strategy

- A grouping of best practices based on what has been successful in the past

- A quantifiable way to measure success in terms of efficiency, market share, stock value, or similar

Business theory and practice include many useful and valuable concepts, such as learning organizations, agile organizations, intrapreneurship, liberated companies, to name but a few.[2] The gig mindset is compatible with all these approaches. However, it is broader yet more compelling on the individual level. It places you squarely at the heart of these concepts and gives you agency within them.

The gig mindset represents a change in your self-perception, in how you think, in how you relate to others, and in how you work. Any person, at any level in any organization, can think "I have a gig mindset" and work toward enacting it personally and inside their organization.

An engineer at a global industrial company headquartered in Europe I spoke with emphasized what he and colleagues had come to realize about the importance of flexibility and not getting fixed on one method or another:

> We realized quite quickly that there was no one way to bring about change. So, some people were talking about frameworks like lean startup and agile. Other people were talking about liberated companies. Yet others were talking about nonviolent communication. It just seemed to me that there was no right answer. It was whatever people chose and made sense for them.

## WHAT YOU'LL FIND IN THIS BOOK

This book is intended to give you a vision of how you can be instrumental in your organization's evolution—strategically and practically. At the same time, you will be developing as an individual, learning and bringing greater value to the people you work with, and opening up new opportunities for yourself.

In Part 2, "The Future Is at Stake," we look at the potential influence of gig mindsetters, where they act in ways that are good for organizations—often through a kind of civil disobedience—but appear to be against the way the organizations traditionally function. We will see how management misinterprets these behaviors through willful blindness, not seeing the value they bring, and interpreting them as negative rather than positive deviance.

Part 3, "Building Proactive Resilience," shows how the gig mindset builds proactive resilience—essential in our volatile times—and how it is a state of mind based on horizon scanning and adaptive capacity. The gig mindset enables reachability, meaning that everyone is able to reach and be reached, and is necessary for organizations in order to mobilize and act effectively when faced with unexpected events.

Part 4, "Opening Minds and Organizations," is an in-depth look at what I call "openers": ways to trigger new thinking and actionable initiatives to help cultivate a gig-mindset work culture. It covers reverse leadership, accountable decentralization, fast learning, improvisation, and work-life balance.

Part 5, "Investing in the Movers," looks at how organizations can find and keep gig mindsetters—I call them "movers" because they move the organization to new ways of thinking. It covers rethinking what a job is, going beyond the CV, recruitment and evaluation in the gig-mindset era, and ways to liberate talent.

Part 6, "Defining a Perpetual Balance," describes a method you can use in workshop mode to define actions and negotiate agreements with colleagues and managers about your next steps—taking into account the upsides and downsides of the traditional mindset and a gig mindset. It recognizes that the optimum balance between these two approaches is a moving target, and offers a way to navigate it by developing structured thinking rather than endless debate and conflict.

Part 7, "Owning Your Personal Strategy," closes the book with three paths that you—the gig mindsetter—may choose to follow based on your situation in your organization: the advocate path, the compromise path, or the exit path. In this part you will find advice, warnings, and examples.

## Finding your way

This book addresses the needs of three profiles. You may relate to more than one of them. These lists give you a general sense of what the book will bring to you. Every case is different, and the items on your own list once you've started reading may well vary. Case studies and action checklists are provided at different points throughout the book to inspire you, and are listed for easy reference in Appendices A6 and A4 respectively.

### Profile 1. Individual perspective from inside an organization

You will:

- See where you are on the gig-traditional spectrum and how you can develop more gig-mindset traits as part of a personal risk-management strategy.

- Gain a sense of identity, and thereby legitimacy, as you work in gig-mindset ways that may have previously caused you problems.

- See examples and practical ideas that will help you, as a gig mindsetter, overcome obstacles and succeed in bringing positive impact to your organization.

- Be better able to conceptualize and verbalize your contribution to the organization because it may not fall into normal HR categories.

**Profile 2. Department, team, and community managers**
You will:

- Learn how to create conditions for your people to build resilience in themselves as well as within the organization.

- Discover new ways to facilitate learning and sharing within teams and groups.

- See guidelines to consider about how you can help your teams become more autonomous and responsible.

- Understand the benefits of working out loud and see how to organize it.

**Profile 3. Senior managers and leaders**
You will:

- Learn how to develop a personalized narrative about the gig mindset for internal communication.

- See strategic guidance to be considered, along with examples of organizational practices to build a work culture that cultivates the gig mindset.

- Discover a method for navigating the polarities of the gig mindset versus the traditional mindset in order to achieve a flexible, appropriate balance. This will be invaluable as you work to propagate the gig mindset in your organization.

- See, most importantly, how gig-mindset behaviors and attitudes can become part of your personal leadership style.

The research and interviews I conducted for this book were a rich source of discovery for me. I encountered the reality of people on the front lines of change, people with a gig-mindset orientation who shared their personal experiences, both positive and negative, with me. I have attempted to integrate as much of this as possible into *The Gig Mindset Advantage*.

Hopefully, you will be inspired and feel confident as you advance toward the future. My aspiration is that this book serves as a compass that helps you plot your direction. No two readers are likely to follow the same route or even reach the same destination. Enjoy the journey and all the detours it brings along the way!

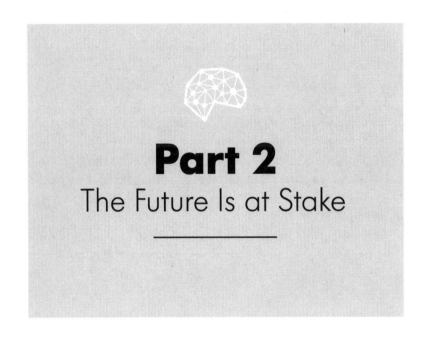

# Part 2
## The Future Is at Stake

## Civil disobedience: An inside job

In my talks, I often describe the gig mindset as "an inside job." We need to change what is happening inside our organizations. But even more, we need to change the conversation and the outlook inside our own heads.

We know there are many things wrong with how organizations work today. Digital transformation has enabled a significant increase in people's capabilities, but it can only take us so far. Work cultures have stagnated, and leadership is still old-school. Most organizations have been through numerous so-called change initiatives involving new standards, new systems, new efficiency models, new business practices, and restructurings. For many employees, the result has been a chaotic workplace where it is unclear what to do, how to do it, and where to find reference materials for guidance.

This internal chaos is made worse by pressures from a volatile external world. Competition is coming from new places: morphing industries; global tech companies; small, fast-moving startups. New technologies, new business, and consumer trends, along with global politics, impact entire industries. Companies are appearing and others disappearing faster today than in the past. All industries and all workers, blue and white collar, manual and intellectual, are impacted.

In these volatile times, people know intellectually that "a job for life" is no longer the case, yet many are not yet planning their professional development in order to be more "marketable internally" should organizational changes require them to change roles or goals. They do not yet have a gig mindset, nor are they aware of its importance.

The rare gig mindsetters inside organizations seem to be less disturbed in this unsettling context. They work differently from others, in ways that are sometimes considered contrary to accepted practices. They have:

- A preference for responsibilities that are defined by skills rather than by hierarchical roles.

- A willingness to take risks; a mindset and readiness to move ahead quickly rather than slowly, without detailed strategizing and planning.

- The ability to act and improvise in real time when they encounter unexpected and unplanned-for events.

To management, these behaviors appear to go against the good of the organization. Yet these gig mindsetters are doing what they believe is in the best interest of the organization. Like people carrying out civil disobedience, defined in political and sociological terms as the nonviolent refusal to comply with regulations of established authorities, gig mindsetters act in what they perceive to be the best interest of their organization—even when this means they will be perceived as troublemakers.

The disconnect comes from the fact that work cultures and leadership have not kept up with the newly emerging behaviors. There is often a big gap.

## A TURNING POINT IN 2015

The gig mindset did not suddenly appear out of the blue. That it is a logical evolution is clear when we take a long-term look at how ways of working have evolved. Detailed input from my 10 years of surveys, which ran to nearly a hundred questions each, have revealed unrecognized truths about organizations, including about skills, leadership styles, work cultures, and challenges people faced in their work. One of the most important observations is that people capabilities have increased tremendously over the past 10 years.

In 2015, three important capabilities came together to set the stage for the emergence of the gig-mindset orientation, and existed in well over half of the organizations I canvassed:

- Being able to find people and expertise through information generated by people and not official HR. This liberated people to interact with others they did not know personally but with whom they could build a relationship.

- Being able to interact through comments on content from other people, including official information from management. This enabled feedback that was visible to others in the organization.

- Being able to connect to people throughout the organization via enterprise social networks. This became a platform for informal communication, creation of work groups, and "enterprise Q&A," asking and answering questions to the "crowd" across the organization.

None of this was possible at scale until new technologies reached large parts of the organization.

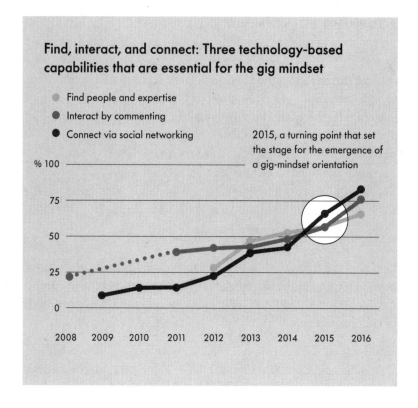

**Find, interact, and connect: Three technology-based capabilities that are essential for the gig mindset**

- Find people and expertise
- Interact by commenting
- Connect via social networking

2015, a turning point that set the stage for the emergence of a gig-mindset orientation

Over the same period, we see that management in most organizations is not keeping pace. Many organizations today are led by well-intentioned high-level people who are defining strategies and action plans based on their long personal experience—what they have seen over their career, and what has worked in the past. Their influence in organizations means that work cultures are lagging behind as well.

At the same time, people in these organizations are using new capabilities to communicate, collaborate and share, and learn. As these capabilities are digital, they go beyond the comfortable organizational silos of the past, weaving a new system of channels and flows. A major collision between the new possibilities and the old way of working is waiting to happen.

# Management attitudes lagging far behind people capabilities

- Find people and expertise
- Interact by commenting
- Connect via social networking

■ Senior management open and participatory

■ People encouraged to give input to business goals, and to challenge business and work practices

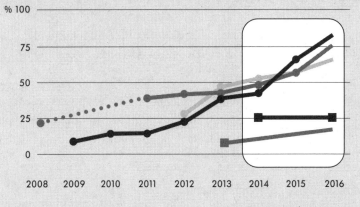

Dangerous distance between people capabilities and management attitudes increasing

## Who are the gig mindsetters?

IN BRIEF: A gig mindsetter has high ambitions for the organization and its future, and looks for ways to make things better and for whatever needs to be disrupted. They bring fundamental new dimensions to how people work.

Gig mindsetters' commitment to the organization is strong and underlies their drive to bring change. A research participant based in the UAE emphasized this:

> The gig mindset includes a level of loyalty to the organization and not the process. Someone with a gig mindset has a willingness to want to make it better.

The engineer I mentioned earlier shared how he and his colleagues strived to bring visibility to how ways of working are changing, through actions he referred to as civil disobedience:

> Some more radical things were coming from the idea that, if we are going to change a company as large as ours, it's not any different to change in society, so why don't we do things like civil disobedience? The idea was actually protesting peacefully in a place on our campus in full visibility of senior management offices. We wanted to call attention to what we are already doing so others can see and join us.

Gig mindsetters with a strong sense of self can potentially influence the people around them. They see issues that others do not see and take action to solve them. They have an outsider perspective because of their interest and participation in external networks and events, and are able to bring this perspective back inside their organization. They cross borders inside the organization and establish horizontal flows of information and energy, as well as flows from the bottom up. They bring new soft skills into the organization, especially those related to autonomy, resilience, stress tolerance, and flexibility.

## BORDER CROSSERS
*Connecting across boundaries and bringing new insights*

A worker with a gig mindset is not a self-centered person focused only on their own goals. They often work across silos in the organization as well as across the hierarchical levels. Horizontality and interdependency are sorely lacking in many organizations. These are, however, defining aspects of the gig mindset. Gig mindsetters work, by nature, across organizational boundaries. They tend to go where they need to go to get the information or support they need to do their work.

A manager in a large global organization in the life sciences sector, who had a strong gig mindset, was leading a change initiative on quality improvements. Of the series of workshops she organized, one was particularly remarkable because the people in the group represented seven levels of hierarchy. Never before had seven levels been in a room together. An older woman in the group, who worked in manufacturing at a relatively low level despite having been there for many years, began to cry quietly. The manager running the workshop discreetly asked her why. The woman, moved by her inclusion in a workshop with senior people, explained:

> Because, after 20 years, this is the first time anyone here has ever asked my opinion about anything.

Another example comes from the public health sector in a European country. The employee designated by management to set up a new cross-organizational research initiative approached the assignment with a gig mindset based on her many years of external networking.

> Part of the reason I was appointed to do what I've been appointed to do is because I network; I know a lot of people. I've been in the organization for seven years. I've also worked in two universities. So I do know a lot of people, and when you need to set something up quickly—for example, patient contact—I know exactly who to phone. I could set up a whole set of patient groups to consult on

the work within a month, and we [could go] all over the country meeting patient groups.

She realized that her ability to work efficiently across silos was not so easy for other people in the organization, or even for herself at times.

But I can see why I've had some of the challenges, because this way of working is being imposed on quite a traditional organization. I could begin to see why some of the tensions had emerged given the framework of traditional- versus gig-mindset thinking.

I'm working right on the boundaries of the organization and have a freedom to work across those business units that maybe other people don't have.

## INSIDE OUTSIDERS
*The clarity and objectivity of the outsider, combined with the in-depth knowledge of the insider*

Gig mindsetters tend to regularly attend or follow external events online. It is second nature to them to want to know what is happening around them, beyond the confines of their organization. They are well placed to bring in external intelligence and insights, to help influence internal decisions.

A government worker in Australia sees the gig mindset as bringing high value to the organization, thanks to the flow of ideas and influence coming to the inside from the outside:

So, if you've got the ideas and you can network, if you're of the ilk that you can go out and learn new things, you can research new things, then you can bring that back and improve the organization just tremendously. So that's where I see that the gig mindset is the way to go.

It is not always clear-cut if you are an insider or outsider. You can be perceived as a source of external expertise even when you're inside an organization. But because you are, in fact, an insider, you know the organization well. If you have developed specific, uncommon expertise, you may well be perceived as an external expert because of your knowledge and skills that are outside the known scope of the workforce. A digital specialist in a Geneva-based world organization explained how he, although an insider, was perceived as an external expert:

> When I'm invited to a conference, it's a sign that people are willing to listen to what I have to say. This brings me more credibility— makes me more the "expert" internally... When I went to New York for two months to work with a different division in our organization, I was brought in as a consultant—they wanted my expert view—to challenge them, and we had a lot of lively discussions. My mandate was clearly to be an adviser—they brought me, an internal colleague, on board instead of an external consultant because they perceived me as a source of external advice.

A mid-career manager in India explained how his way of working recently changed and why he decided to position himself internally as an external adviser:

> Knowing that, in the future, permanent jobs will be replaced with gigs and projects based on skills and aptitude has enabled me to adopt a consultant mindset, where I can see things from within the organization with the eyes of an outsider. It allows me to see things in a new light.

**DETECTORS**
*Getting what others do not see onto the radar*

Gig mindsetters are confident they can bring value to the organization in ways that other people, especially their managers, do not necessarily see. They create ad hoc projects and teams, assuming responsibility for the outcome. They are ambitious and willing to risk failure if it means they have learned something and helped the project advance. A woman I have known for close to 10 years and who has been a manager in a large industrial organization and in a retail company—two very different sectors—observed similarities in how gig mindsetters operate in both cases:

> People with a gig mindset are not solitary cowboys roaming the wild west of organizations. They often detect new, unseen issues, then work to solve them. They have charisma and know how to bring people together around a project, around a mission. They often work undercover, in the gaps between official initiatives, bringing life to spaces in the organization where previously there was nothing. When the project takes shape and is sustainable, often someone else takes over because the organization prefers a visible project manager with a clear, understood profile.

Gig mindsetters don't just make problems visible but do something about them. They open eyes and trigger change in specific ways, solving problems that had not yet been noticed, as a research participant from Canada explained:

> Another opportunity for people who work with the gig mindset is when they can get at projects that might fall down in priority in a traditional setup, where you're waiting for approval or a response. A person with a gig mindset might be able to maneuver and get a project set up, initiate or be the catalyst to get at those projects that might be lower in priority otherwise.
>
> Once they get ownership of that and get it moving, it perhaps becomes priority in the eyes of top management.
>
> Particularly if they're working on projects that start off as something that was between the cracks and you come to the realization that it's not a between-the-cracks project. This is going to fundamentally address a problem that we have that we did not see coming.

## INFLUENCERS
*Influencing others by the way you see yourself*

Behavior of peers is the highest change influencer in organizations. The way you see yourself influences the way you act, which in turn influences the behavior of others. In 10 years of annual surveys about the internal digital work environment, I have seen, year after year, that one of the highest change influencers in organizations is "behavior of my colleagues."

If you see yourself as a person with a gig mindset, you will interpret events differently than will a person with a traditional mindset. Your peers will be influenced by your behavior. Resistance and setbacks will be perceived as challenges to overcome, and the way you handle them will influence others. A person with a traditional mindset may become discouraged and interpret the same events as defeat. You, on the other hand, can influence others through your own behavior. The starting point is your confidence in your own capabilities.

Psychologist Albert Bandura developed the concept of self-efficacy—how you perceive yourself and what you believe you can do with what you have in your given circumstances. It is not the skills you have but your belief in your own ability to influence change. People with high self-efficacy, as is the case with many gig mindsetters, show the following traits:

1. Taking on difficult tasks, seeing them as challenges and staying the course even when it gets difficult.

2. Continuing despite failure, and transforming it into a learning experience.

3. Remaining sure of oneself, maintaining energy and enthusiasm in difficult surroundings, such as management indifference or unreasonable demands from others.

According to Bandura, when a small number of highly credible individuals show certain behaviors, they have the ability to influence people around them. Indeed, the behavior of other people is a key factor in relation to change.[1]

An experienced VP specialized in knowledge development described how people with a gig mindset become influencers and play a role of bridging across silos and organizational gaps:

> We see people who are more gig mindset as kind of weird outliers, but what they're really good at is building their influence. They practice it externally because they try to stay networked to peers outside the organization. Then they take that skill and develop it internally as well. I think that starts to build up a sense of being an internal influencer, and they're always seeking to explain their perspective on whatever project they're working on. I think that, over time, that makes them a bridging personality. They bridge between functions or between silos or across projects, and those can be very key elements in an organization.
>
> They build a diverse network and have the ability to cut across silos and against organizational gaps. You work from gig to gig and, over time, you become an influencer in areas of the organization. That might not have happened if you had just been customer service rep 3, customer service rep 2, customer service rep 1, then customer service manager, for example.

## CARRIERS OF NEW SKILLS
*Emerging soft skills now seen as business critical*

The importance of new skills, primarily soft skills, is gradually being recognized in our era, where "the way we used to do it" is no longer effective. People with a gig mindset embody several of the emerging soft skills that organizations are realizing they need.

Coincidentally, the gig-mindset traits that the advisory board and I identified for our 2018 mindset research (listed in Appendix A1) are very close to the skills identified in *The Future of Jobs Report*, published by the World Economic Forum (WEF) in the same year. The differences between the WEF 2016 and 2018 reports are striking. New skills were added in 2018; others were defined more explicitly.

Two categories from the 2018 report are especially relevant to the gig mindset. The first is "creativity, originality, and initiative," and, as redefined in 2018, includes five skills: initiative, creativity, responsibility, autonomy, and originality. A second and new category appeared in 2018, which also reflects the gig mindset: "resilience, stress tolerance, and flexibility." It includes three skills: adaptability, self-control, and stress tolerance.[2] These last three skills lead us to the topic of work-life balance, discussed in Part 4, "Opening Minds and Organizations."

At the beginning of this section, we saw how work cultures have stagnated and many leaders are still old-school, far from being in an open and participatory mode of work. In the next section we will see why this is so.

## From willful blindness to positive deviance

IN BRIEF: As the small segment of gig-mindset employees with the behaviors we have described begins to make itself seen and heard, we have a clash building up. There are reasons for resistance to the gig-mindset way of working, and it is important to understand them in order to overcome them.

Indrajit Gupta, an India-based analyst, editor, and business journalist, cofounder and director of Founding Fuel, has seen the resistance of senior management firsthand:

I think it's a form of blindness, a case of willful blindness. Some senior people are unable to step back and see why they're losing relevance, especially if they've been successful in the past. But if you get caught up in operations, and if you think that you can shut out the world and keep doing what you're doing forever and ever, and follow the processes that you've done all your life and that you'll continue to remain relevant, it's a fallacy. If you look at any industry, in India or in the US, the mortality of companies is frightening. But why don't more people get it, then? That's the key question.

The term "willful blindness" is not used casually. It originates in the field of law and refers to situations where people are responsible for things they should have or could have known but apparently do not, or at least claim not to.[3]

What is making it so difficult for people, especially those in senior positions, to see what is happening today? We will look at six common mental or emotional traps detrimental to the future of organizations:

- Pride in past success
- Dependence on best practices and benchmarking
- Fear of losing power
- Fear of speed
- A false sense of safety in silos
- Living in filter bubbles

Many of these are fear-based, with people clinging to the past and afraid to move into the uncertainty of the future.

## PRIDE IN PAST SUCCESS
*Blinders in a fast-changing world*

People who have worked for 10 or more years to reach where they are in the hierarchy are often not at ease with someone who challenges the status quo and questions how the system works. People with a traditional mindset believe there is no reason to interfere with something that has worked well in the past and appears to continue to do so.

Gig mindsetters, on the other hand, are frustrated when they cannot advance, cannot contribute to the future of their organizations. These reactions when their senior managers, based on past experiences and worldviews, do not welcome experimentation are normal.

A highly experienced organizational strategist and consultant with decades of work inside and outside India highlighted a major problem when I asked him why management discourages a gig mindset:

They are extremely procedural. They insist "This is the way it has always been done." They are blind to the changes that are taking place in a social context.

The reason people "don't get it" is that the approach worked in the past. That's exactly the problem, as a manager based in the US told me:

> Senior leadership can have an "if it's not broken, don't fix it" mindset that makes new ideas and ways of working a much tougher sell.

Others see that change is essential but do not know how to go about it. The idea of "starting from scratch" is appealing but not realistic for many. Developing a startup mindset is a good way to begin. An external strategy adviser explained how hard it is for senior directors to see how to change their practices:

> Today, I talked with an executive director who sits on the board of a general insurance company. The company is grabbing some new market shares, which is great. But there are market spaces they're leaving weakened and they don't know how to address them because it means going back to being entrepreneurial all over again. Starting from scratch; starting with a startup mindset. It's very hard, because they have become rigid. Their own success has sown the seeds of destruction because they're unable to see new opportunities. They're so used to doing work in a certain way. I think the whole siloed way of working and the lack of a cross-functional orientation makes it harder and harder. I asked [the senior director] some fairly tough questions, but he was candid enough. He said, "Look, our folks in HR just simply don't have value at all. Our CEO gets it, but HR is into tick-box training, and they don't understand the needs of business at all."

In this case, ironically, the biggest barrier to new business is HR, the very department that should be working with people to facilitate

the changes they need to get new business. In general, the HR function is the most variable and least predictable among all the key
organizational players. HR may be strategic, may manage knowledge
sharing and skills building, or may simply handle administration
and payroll. I called them the joker card in my digital organization
research report of 2008.[4] As I said six years later in the 2014 report,
HR is often stuck between what management wants them to do and
what they need to be doing for the people. HR is the one function that
can connect management words with real actions.[5] One gig-mindset
research participant said that "high-level managers say they believe
in many of the gig-mindset values but in reality they pivot the organizational structure to get rid of those very people."

This exemplifies the pitfall of having so much pride in the past
that, despite their words, they are unable to face the reality of what
the words mean.

## DEPENDENCE ON BEST PRACTICES AND BENCHMARKING
*Leaning on the past, not leaning into the future*

Focusing on the future does not mean forgetting the past. It does not
mean ignoring traditional benchmarking and best practices that others are following. It does mean looking forward and not using the
past as your only guide to the future—and not assuming that your
traditional competitors are the most relevant organizations to watch
today. Corporate strategist and author C.K. Prahalad emphasized
the importance of looking forward rather than backward when he
wrote that the forgetting curve was more important than the learning curve, and advised organizations to look for *next* practices rather
than studying best practices.[6]

One problem with the way most organizations do benchmarking
is their comparison of what they are doing with what their peer organizations are doing. Today, it is less certain that your traditional peers
will still be your competitors tomorrow. The global tech giants are
entering new markets. Amazon has moved into retail grocery shop-
ping; Google is active in the automotive industry with self-driving.

What some of us may have missed is that traditional companies are beginning to do the same. For example, Sony, a giant in electronics and entertainment, has started to produce electric parts for automobiles. Fujifilm, the camera company, has a brand of cosmetics, Astalift, based on antioxidants used in its core business.[7]

It is more likely that competition will arise from a global giant like Google, Facebook, or Amazon, or, conversely, from a small startup that no one has heard of before. Competition may also come from legacy companies, but in a different industry. It has become hard to predict where and when your next competitor will appear.

## FEAR OF LOSING POWER
*Weakening of the hierarchical crutch*

People fear losing what they have. For senior leaders, the premise of the gig mindset disrupts long-held views about themselves, how they work, and how they are being challenged, indirectly, by people throughout their organization who are beginning to act independently of hierarchies and taking initiatives that are not preapproved. The engineer who earlier talked about civil disobedience pinpointed the challenge:

> The gig mindset and flexible way of working vastly undermine the existential purpose of traditional management, managerial control, or positions for individuals who may have been working for 20 or more years. Because they've become so attached to the idea of being a manager and what that means, it's incredibly destabilizing to imagine that suddenly their role as they lived it for so long is no longer needed.

When recruiting and making hiring decisions, people who value power based on hierarchy are likely to hire new people who show respect for the status quo. They are unlikely to threaten the "way things are done here" with new ideas and new ways of working. A similar emphasis on losing power came from a government employee in Australia:

The behaviors listed in the survey for the traditional mindset and the gig mindset confirm why it is difficult for organizations to work collaboratively. Those that seek to maintain the status quo are increasingly working with a growing number seeking change. The tension is unresolved. Power remains with those who seek to maintain the status quo and is used to promote those of a like mind who are not a threat.

## FEAR OF SPEED
*Careful and cautious, step by slow step*

We all know that cultures and work practices reinforce themselves. This is part of the traditional mindset: most people prefer proven and approved methods and maintaining stability and consistency in work habits. This mindset is most often found at the highest levels of organizations and people with it are uncomfortable, threatened even, when faced with others working with a gig mindset. They want to put the brakes on, slow down the train.

Survey participants were asked to rate their behaviors on a 5-point scale from 1 (highly traditional mindset) to 5 (highly gig mindset) for each of the eight gig-mindset traits. (You'll find the table of traits in Appendix A1.) People with a strong gig mindset, those with an average score of 4 or higher, perceive change happening much faster externally than internally.[8] They tend to be impatient with slow, methodical approaches because, with their extensive networking and awareness of the speed of change in the external world, they are motivated to move fast themselves.

In contrast, people who are less gig-mindset oriented perceive change happening inside and outside at approximately the same speed. They feel that everything is moving along just fine.

Data show that people in the higher group reflect a 25 percentage-point lead in the speed of external change compared with internal change, whereas only 4 percent of people with a lower gig-mindset score show that difference.

These are the people who have ambitions for their organization. They are monitoring external activity and what is happening in the

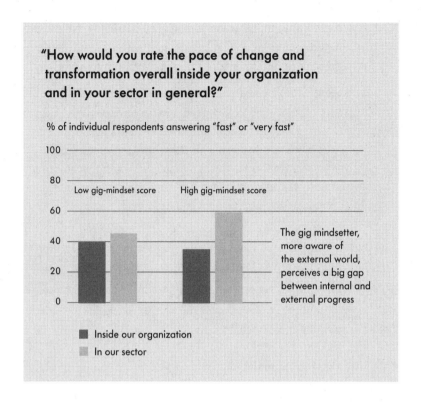

"How would you rate the pace of change and transformation overall inside your organization and in your sector in general?"

% of individual respondents answering "fast" or "very fast"

Low gig-mindset score    High gig-mindset score

The gig mindsetter, more aware of the external world, perceives a big gap between internal and external progress

■ Inside our organization
■ In our sector

market. They are not necessarily right. They may be too pessimistic about the pace of internal change or too optimistic about the pace of external change. It may be a case of the grass being greener on the other side of the fence. But that is less important than their looking at the big picture with a critical eye, concerned that their organization may be lagging behind. They want to mobilize people and move ahead to deal with challenges. As a very senior IT director, exceptionally gig-minded in his work and near retirement, said:

> It's transform or die, basically; there's no doubt about it. One of our main objectives is to be the leader in the energy transition world, and we're doing everything we can to keep ahead of the game in that.

This senior manager's attitude is uncommon. A senior technical expert in a large global company headquartered in Europe explained how, after building an internal social platform, he and his colleagues attempted to change mindsets in their organization, and how they did not feel a need to involve senior management, nor HR:

> I don't know if it was ever conscious on my side, but I was not really in touch with any senior executives. I didn't want to be. I thought, "I have a huge platform now to reach lots of people, have lots of discussion; let's see if we can shake the tree a little bit." It never really occurred to me to reach out to senior managers, to be honest with you. It was like we don't really need them at this point in time. We can just crack on and do stuff.

The people pushing to bring about change often do not involve senior management, feeling that their participation is unnecessary. In these cases, senior management may have a sense of losing control because the traditional steps for agreeing to objectives and strategy, and for setting up projects and associated schedules, are shortened drastically or skipped altogether.

## A FALSE SENSE OF SAFETY IN SILOS
*Protected by illusions of independence in one's own space*

"My silo is my neighborhood. But my neighborhood is part of a city." This was the way an intranet strategy manager in a global industrial company I spoke with made people in his company stop and think about the difference between closed silos and open silos. It's the city part that most people forget about. It also makes sense to go beyond that, as the city is part of a country, which is part of the world.

The weight of silos and internal power struggles can be a burden. This was the case for a man who left his retail organization a year or so after joining:

> We have flex workdays, as we are working from home, but since people still work in silos, nothing is shared openly. This makes it extremely difficult to find people with a specific area of expertise. Believe it or not, sometimes people don't even say that they are connected and listening in to a conference call.

Horizontal flows and interactions are often unofficial, and not supported or even facilitated by processes. Even when the value of cross-stream collaboration is recognized, it is not always integrated into the systems. It may be the informal way of working, but once it requires cross-organizational processes and budgets, it stops—as a manager in a global company from Sweden described:

> Decisions are distributed to the edge of the organizations. Here, the organizations are very strong—stronger than processes and projects. On the other hand, there is an unwritten agreement to help each other to solve the problem. This culture creates freedom to act, and I know hundreds of examples of people who do things on a regular basis outside their own area and out of their assignment scope to help people and organizations. It works really well to solve problems, but this is an informal culture. It's strangely okay with management if we start initiatives as long as we talk about working in general. But when it comes to financing and ownership, which is when the responsibility must be formalized, then we are stopped. We don't really have any cross-functional processes or organizations. It makes it difficult for organizations or processes to reach agreement on cross-functional initiatives.

The fact that cross-organizational flows exist, even if they are informal, is a good start. Hopefully, the gig mindsetters in the organization will manage to pierce the functional barriers enough to get some flows going across the silos. From the neighborhoods to the city!

## LIVING IN FILTER BUBBLES
*Isolated in the center, disconnected from the edges of the organization*

The people on the edges of organizations, especially those who are customer-facing, see more of the external world than do those inside the corporation, especially senior management, who often live in filter bubbles, hearing and seeing only what conforms to their views. Unfortunately, those on the edge are often forgotten or the last to be consulted when digital and other strategies are being defined.

I discussed this with a headquarters-based board member in a large organization a couple years ago. He told me he saw no reason to change how people work because the company has always been successful. He said it with a straight face, deadly serious. And it's true that, up to that point, the company was a leader in the business.

The organization had invited me to speak at a workshop where people came together from various countries. Team after team spoke about their challenges, the competition in their markets, and their ideas about how to renovate their approach to digital.

Ideas flowed around the room, and as people talked, I watched the board member's face. He didn't speak, but I got the distinct impression he was getting a wake-up call. In his case, the external influence was from his own company, though not from headquarters where he spent his time but from customer-facing teams in the global group. So, in this case, the voice of the external world came to him via the people on the ground, who lived the external reality daily, people he did not normally come into contact with in his everyday work.

A business journalist in India spoke about watching the outliers, too often ignored by managers, and the need to integrate external awareness into everyday work:

> Most management teams reflect on a regular basis, such as once a year off-site. There's a lot of song and dance, and then they go back to doing what they did. The problem is they need to continually question presumptions and see what's happening at the boundaries, at the edges of their business, look at the outliers who are chipping away without their realizing it.

Putting faith primarily in best practices is an approach still taught in some business schools and higher educational institutions, where case studies, by definition from the past, are analyzed to learn how to operate today. Not everyone agrees with using this approach and some believe a more reliable approach is one based on scenarios, which forces students to gather information and develop their own perspectives.[9]

Which approach—case studies or scenarios—builds external awareness? Which best suits the era of uncertainty? Probably a combination of both. But just like with organizations where the balance between the traditional mindset and the gig mindset tips too far toward the traditional, training and learning sessions for managers tend to be too dependent on best practices and case studies and too rarely based on creative scenario-planning sessions. The second are much harder for instructors to facilitate, just as the gig mindset is harder for management to cultivate. But both are essential to develop creative, future-leaning managers who, later, will be prepared to lead their organizations through changing, volatile times.

### QUESTIONS TO ASK: WILLFUL BLINDNESS AND EXTERNAL AWARENESS

Lack of awareness of the external world has a large impact on willful blindness. If you don't see it, how can you be responsible? Even if you should have seen it. The following questions offer suggestions for increasing external awareness:

❶ Do we have a network of advisers from various organizations, including subject matter experts, industry analysts, and external peers?

❷ Are most of our internal online communities cross-organizational and multi-functional, bringing together different perspectives?

❸ Do some of our online communities include external people?

❹ Do we have systems for continuously getting and sharing input from the external world?

❺ Are people encouraged to participate in external conferences, events, and communities during work hours?

❻ Are costs (up to a certain ceiling) for these events covered by the organization without a need for preapproval?

❼ Do we invite external people, such as thought leaders and peers in other organizations, to internal events so they can share their experiences and challenge our practices?

## RESILIENCE FROM POSITIVE DEVIANCE

Managers, and people in general, perceive certain gig-mindset behaviors with apprehension or even fear. This is a classic case of positive deviance: perceiving something good as being dangerous. Positive deviants are people whose behavior is perceived as negative, deviant, even harmful, but who end up with positive outcomes thanks to that behavior.[10]

The table below lists five gig-mindset behaviors and how they can be perceived simultaneously as deviance and as positive deviance, depending on the observer. The positive deviance perception shows how these behaviors help build resilience. We'll explore each behavior in Part 3, "Building Proactive Resilience."

| THE BEHAVIOR | PERCEPTIONS | |
| --- | --- | --- |
| | Deviance against the organization | Positive deviance for the organization, building resilience |
| Experimental, unapproved initiatives | Undisciplined, unmanageable, disrespectful of established ways of working | Discoveries within a broad framework; new services and markets |
| Team-building across silos based on skills rather than roles | A threat to hierarchy; loss of control by silo owners | Faster and more comprehensive results; increased impact thanks to diversity of ideas and skills |
| Openness and working out loud | Risky because confidential information may be exposed | Enriching because of broader input and faster reactions, early anticipation and resolution of potential issues |
| Challenging the status quo | Lack of respect for management | Exploring new ways of working and serving customers |

| THE BEHAVIOR | PERCEPTIONS | |
|---|---|---|
| External networking and continually learning new skills | Being self-centered and individualistic | Building awareness of what is happening, not just with known competitors but with the current and potential customer base |

## TOO MUCH CONTROL MEANS VULNERABILITY

Because gig-mindset behaviors trigger negative reactions in most organizations, management tends to control or repress them. Ironically, the more management resists, the more they lose control. In *Resilience Thinking: Sustaining Ecosystems and People in a Changing World*,[11] Brian Walker and David Salt explain that when organizations attempt to maintain systems and work methods they are accustomed to, they can end up becoming more vulnerable. This is because they are unprepared for future disturbances and will not be in control when the unexpected happens. Suppressing or weakening behaviors such as those listed in the table above leave the organization vulnerable when there are sudden changes. This is because people who carry out unapproved initiatives and experiments are likely to be those who come up with actionable ideas in times of stress.

Similarly, people who are accustomed to working in cross-organizational teams with responsibilities defined according to skills—rather than according to official titles and roles—will know others with the needed skills whom they can mobilize when a disruption occurs. People who work openly will produce results faster because of the broader source of input and ideas from others outside the official team. People who are comfortable challenging the status quo will bring new perspectives and ideas when decisions must be made in new, unfamiliar situations. Lastly, people who do extensive external networking may well have contacts outside the organization who can be called on for support and potential joint efforts to solve a problem. These behaviors are part of organizational resilience, which is the subject of the following Part 3, "Building Proactive Resilience."

## CASE STUDY: Behaviors that transform

Merck KGaA, Darmstadt, Germany, is a science and technology company operating across healthcare, life science, and performance-materials with some fifty-seven thousand employees in 66 countries.

### Seeing far ahead: A future-oriented Competency Model, five years old and still growing

Merck KGaA, Darmstadt, Germany, has developed a future-oriented Competency Model as a framework to guide processes and decision-making across the organization. This is a highly structured yet simple and clear framework that encourages, validates, and rewards many gig-mindset behaviors. It offers a foundation for a work culture where gig-mindset behaviors can be adapted and cultivated when and where appropriate.

In 2015, the company developed a behavior-based Competency Model through a year-long series of workshops that took place around the world. It was championed by a new CEO, who wanted to drive an agenda on innovation, technology, and digital transformation. The HR team behind the model worked with both the CEO and the board to ensure that the model was both aspirational and aligned to the company's strategy. The result was an actionable blend between bottom-up, top-down, and horizontal flows of information and the convergence of values across the whole organization. The model is based on six themes:

1. Purposeful: Make great things happen
2. Future-oriented: Shape the future
3. Innovative: Take calculated risks
4. Results-driven: Take ownership
5. Collaborative: Have an inclusive mindset
6. Empowering: Inspire people to reach their full potential

Each theme has four actionable subthemes, each starting with a verb. For example, *future-oriented* is divided into *anticipate opportunities*, *be entrepreneurial*, *go digital*, and *apply technology*. And *empowering* is divided into *foster talents*, *develop people*, *give vision*, and *share emotions*.

Jennifer O'Lear, chief diversity officer and head of Engagement and Inclusion, was one of the leaders of the initiative: "We use it at a high messaging level to communicate about how the company is changing. At the same time, it is embedded in all of the HR programs and processes in terms of assessments and expected behaviors." She added: "The model has had staying power, and people refer to it without looking it up."

## EMPOWERING DEVELOPMENT TEAMS

Britta Paschen, head of Global Evidence and Value Strategy Development for Biopharma, talked to me about how the Competency Model empowered global development teams and led them to *take ownership* of their work, one of the themes of the model. The role of these global development teams is to lead early research up to clinical studies, then to regulatory approval and (pre-)launch. This process can last more than 10 years. In the past, development teams had to report progress and get approvals from various steering committees across the organization at frequent points along the timeline. Today, they are encouraged to manage themselves, in an entrepreneur-like spirit. They now have only three touch points with top management in order to get their funding. At regular intervals along the process they can convoke sounding boards with experts at different levels and different parts of the company, such as safety, manufacturing, efficacy, and market access. This lets them get feedback and learn from internal and external experts while still taking ownership of the final decision.

As Paschen said: "The more you control, the more you create the learned helplessness. Today, fewer controls have increased motivation and openness within the teams. People have controversial discussions to define what might be the right way forward, because there are always different options and scenarios, with pros and cons. If people disagree within a team, it is seen as a source of creativity, not criticism."

Challenging the status quo and encouraging a spirit of contradiction are key to building a gig-mindset work culture. This already existed in isolated parts of Merck KGaA, Darmstadt, Germany, but the Competency Model reinforced it and brought it into the official language.

## GETTING THE RIGHT PEOPLE

Jit Saini, head of Medical Affairs EMEA, explained how elements of the Competency Model have been used to develop an interview guide, to bring the right talent into the company. Medical Affairs is responsible for taking a regulatory-approved product and ensuring eligible patients can benefit from that drug in clinical practice. It is an ethically driven function, with a focus on patients as opposed to sales. "There are many ways you can check technical expertise, but we need to also make sure we are hiring the right people, bringing the right values and behaviors to the table."

One theme of the model is *Have an inclusive mindset*. I asked Saini how he explored this in a job interview. He explained: "I give an example, such as mentioning that we have created country-level R&D councils and need to be sure we have all the right voices at the table. Which functions should be included? A candidate's answer gives me a sense of how the person sees the roles of others and whether the person understands how an R&D group can work together and how interlinked our efforts really are."

Another theme is *Shape the future*. Saini asks job candidates how they think about the future: "How do you put yourself in the patients' shoes, people who have cancer, infertility, multiple sclerosis, and so on, and understand their needs? How would you then champion R&D to produce treatments for these diseases? How would you help commercial teams understand why this is the right future strategy for patients?" Tough questions indeed, but questions that require thought and an exploratory mindset, which is part of the gig mindset.

## HOW HAS THE COMPETENCY MODEL LASTED SO LONG?

Most corporate initiatives are short-lived. Value and vision statements live primarily on paper. The Competency Model of Merck KGaA, Darmstadt, Germany, on the other hand, has lasted since 2015 and is actively appropriated by people in the organization.

It is a framework that is structured enough to embed a culture, but flexible enough not to become stiff and unusable. In a global company present in 66 countries, a model has to be adaptable. Saini summed it up: "It can be tailored to what you need it to be, without compromising what it is meant to be."

> **Results-driven:** *Take ownership* is the slogan in *Results-driven*, one of the six primary themes of the Competency Model created by Merck KGaA, Darmstadt, Germany. These are the actionable behaviors for each level of the company:
>
> Foundation (everyone): Fulfills own commitments and admits when mistakes occur.
>
> Manager 1: Takes appropriate action to ensure reliable team results are delivered.
>
> Manager 2: Recognizes responsibility for own team performance and takes accountability for mistakes or underachievement of team members.
>
> Manager 3: Promotes giving ownership to the lowest level possible by encouraging delegation and avoiding micromanagement.
>
> Manager 4: Provides ample opportunities for team members to own their assigned projects and progress.

**Manager 5:** Educates managers that they need to provide the resources people need to own their job (e.g., clear role description, control over task, tools, training, mentors).

**Executive:** Shapes an environment in which it is easy for employees to take responsibility for their decisions and actions by exemplifying this through own behavior.

---

This case is based on interviews and information from Jennifer O'Lear, chief diversity officer and head of Engagement and Inclusion; Britta Paschen, head of Global Evidence and Value Strategy Development for Biopharma; and Jit Saini, head of Medical Affairs EMEA.
www.emdgroup.com/en/company.html

# Part 3
## Building Proactive Resilience

---

**Being resilient** in the face of nonstop change is a never-ending challenge. The rules of the game change as competition comes from new companies "born on the Net," as well as from players in industries that were not considered competitors in the past. Technological advances are disrupting all industries and impacting all ages of workers, both manual and intellectual.

Resilience has been studied by scientists, psychologists, academics, and management thinkers over many years. It is a dedicated field in environmental science and human psychology and has been integrated into management theory research. (See "Recommended Reading," at the back of the book, for a list of interesting sources.) Each researcher has their own definitions and list of characteristics.

Resilience has two sides: organizational and individual. Let's address the first. (The second is covered in a later section entitled "Work-Life Balance.")

As a starting point is a conversation I had with Kavi Arasu, director of Learning and Change at Founding Fuel, in India. Based on what he has seen in over 20 years of experience working with large international companies in Europe and Asia, he said that converging changes are raising critical challenges for everyone:

The nature of work in itself is shifting. I've been through several cycles of change, but I've never been through such parallel streams of change as are running now—generational differences, multiplied by technology, multiplied by the nature of the market. This is very difficult for organizations to fathom. And greater technology change is coming. It's so massive that it constantly requires re-engineering, reimagining, and adaption of the mind, which is not happening. That's a huge challenge as well. Not everybody has been able to adapt.

## A state of mind

IN BRIEF: Resilience is more than just being able to get through a crisis. Making it through once is not enough. It is highly likely there will be more and greater disruption in both the short and long term. Being proactively resilient means using a crisis to revitalize ways of working that will make it easier to face the next disruption with serenity. This means using the experience to transform into something new and stronger.

The British Standards Institution (also known as the BSI Group) visualizes organizational resilience as a race that has "no finishing line" and says that it is a process of continual improvement essential for organizations to survive and prosper.[1] Others describe resilience as a state of mind, a way of working that is continually on. D. Christopher Kayes underlines the importance of proactive resilience when he says that it is not just about solving problems today but about how to avoid or alleviate them in the future.[2]

Gary Hamel and Liisa Välikangas, in the *Harvard Business Review*, go so far as to say that proactive resilience is more important for success than is improving your current business activities. You need to be able to reinvent your business models and adapt your strategies as circumstances change.[3]

Resilience is a priority for competitive advantage, but a weakness in most organizations. The British Standards Institution identified 16 elements that make up organizational resilience and then asked senior business leaders to rate the impact each has on long-term success, and how the leaders perceived their own performance of each element. Comparing the results of the British Standards Institution's 2017 report with that of 2019 shows a significant shift in perceptions, both in impact and performance. Two elements especially relevant to our exploration of the gig mindset are *horizon scanning* and *adaptive capacity.*

- Horizon scanning: systematically observing trends and developments around you in order to identify challenges and opportunities.

- Adaptive capacity: the skills and strategies of individuals and organizations to respond to change in the environment around them.

Companies have realized how important these two elements are, the senior business leaders rating their impact on the organizations much higher in 2019 than in 2017. On the other hand, the leaders' self-assessment was low in both areas. The British Standards Institution website offers access to several of its past reports on organizational resilience, where you can see its observations directly.[4]

## Horizon scanning

Business leaders, as mentioned, recognized in 2019 that a critical requirement for resilience, that of horizon scanning, was weak. How can you possibly stay ahead of the competition if you don't see what is out there, and have low awareness of your situation in the larger context? I remember a conversation I had in Stockholm nearly 10 years ago while with a technology expert in his nearly self-driving car (it was impressive to feel it automatically slow down every time we came close to a car ahead of us on the highway). As we moved slowly through the rush-hour traffic, I had plenty of time to get his views on why Nokia had lost leadership in the mobile phone market. I had worked with Nokia several times in 2001 and 2003. Their headquarters in Espoo, outside Helsinki, was a magnificent building, tall and transparent, with glass walls and an elevator in the center. The lobby had dozens of displays of beautiful mobile phones, their designs the ultimate in usability at that time.

I asked my companion what he thought had happened. What had changed for Nokia? His answer, in short, was that they had not seen Android coming. And they missed the smartphone emergence led by Apple, thinking their brand was stronger. Ego? Lack of horizon scanning? That it was unable to make the move to smartphones is an interesting twist to the history of a 150-year-old company that had shown adaptive capacity over decades by evolving from making paper and then rubber galoshes to making mobile phones. What might the results have been if Nokia had had a gig-mindset-based work culture—one that integrated the core strength of high external awareness through "outsider" perspectives and extensive networking within and beyond the organization?

What this example highlights is that a lack of horizon scanning was very likely what destroyed a potential leadership position in the emerging smartphone market.[5]

## Adaptive capacity

It does little good to scan the horizon for new trends if you are not able to then adapt your goals and actions. This appears to be the case for many companies. My research between 2013 and 2018 with over three hundred organizations showed they did not feel their adaptive capacity was high. I asked the leaders of these organizations to rate, using a 5-degree scale, their agreement or disagreement with the statement "Our organization can respond rapidly to major events or transitions: market changes, competition, economy downturns, environmental or disaster events."

The low levels of agreement (represented by the dark gray bars at the bottom of the chart below) illustrate that significant

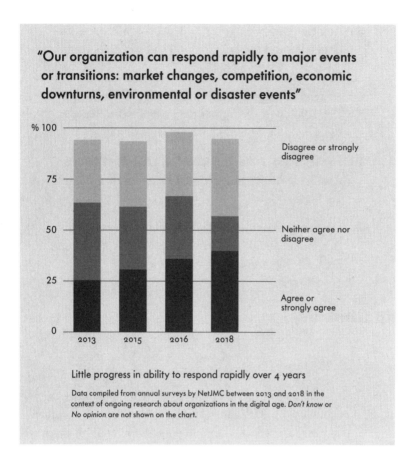

"Our organization can respond rapidly to major events or transitions: market changes, competition, economic downturns, environmental or disaster events"

Little progress in ability to respond rapidly over 4 years

Data compiled from annual surveys by NetJMC between 2013 and 2018 in the context of ongoing research about organizations in the digital age. *Don't know* or *No opinion* are not shown on the chart.

vulnerabilities still exist today. Improvement between 2013 and 2018 was minimal. There's a lot of progress to be made.

### QUESTIONS TO ASK: ADAPTIVE CAPACITY

Adaptive capacity is strong in an organization when it is easy to mobilize people quickly, and they can be counted on to take initiatives and act appropriately as the situation requires. It includes people's ability to improvise. And it means that people are able to reach and communicate with others easily. (Reach-ability is discussed in more detail in the next section.)

❶ Are there easy ways to find people with specific expertise and experience, and put together teams for projects at short notice?

❷ Do teams and people have a high degree of autonomy that allows them to define their goals and ways of working?

❸ Are teams and people enabled to act and, when necessary, shortcut enterprise processes in order to advance rapidly?

❹ Do you have communities beyond the traditional functional and project groups that deal with topics such as problem-solving?

## Reachability

IN BRIEF: Reachability means that people anywhere in the organization can be contacted directly and individually in near real time. This is important for cultivating a gig-mindset work culture. People can communicate and interact with others beyond their physical workplace. It means ideas and initiatives that originate in one place can reach across the organization to all interested people. Reachability is a requirement for resilience.

When an organization has reachability, gig-mindset-oriented workers, wherever they are in the organization, can share their ideas and initiatives with others. They are less isolated.

When there is a problem to solve, a challenge to confront, all people in the organization can contribute ideas. Whether in a small company with a few teleworkers or a global organization with thousands of people around the world, reachability breeds resilience. It facilitates multidirectional flows of communication, is a natural antidote against the dominance of a traditional mindset, and, above all, makes it possible to get all hands on board fast when a crisis hits.

Most organizations do not have sufficient reachability.

# Reachability enables resilience and the ability to mobilize in crisis

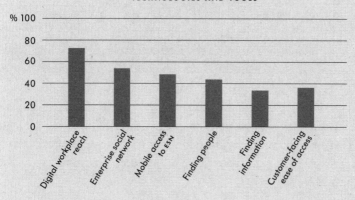

TECHNOLOGIES AND TOOLS

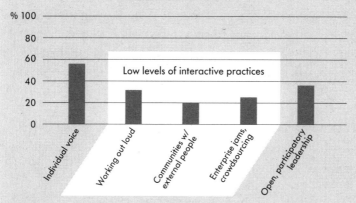

WORK PRACTICES AND BEHAVIORS

Data collected from 300 organizations around the world, 10th annual research:
The Organization in the Digital Age, 2016.

Attaining reachability requires digital technologies and interactive work practices. The digital divide we see in many organizations among different segments of workers exists because digital and transformation initiatives tend to be driven from the center. The result? Organizations end up off balance. Global viewpoints are favored over local ones; centralized decisions over decentralized. Desk workers have better access to information than deskless workers, as do people at headquarters compared with those working on the edges of the organization.

The technologies that make reachability possible include enterprise-wide social networks, access via mobile devices, people and expertise directories, taxonomies or keywords that help people find information, and security protocols that let people off-site, such as customer-facing teams, access the information and tools they need to do their work.

A second necessity is having interactive work practices in place. This includes working out loud, where people share their work in an ongoing way before actually finishing the project; having communities that include people outside the organization who bring the external voice inside; crowdsourcing activities that enable people from anywhere in the organization to offer their ideas; and finally, open and participatory leadership—senior managers who encourage open discussions and listen to what people say, regardless of their role and level in the organization.

The chart on page 51 shows that the levels of interactive work practices did not reach 50 percent in 2016. Some of these points were surveyed in earlier years, and changes from year to year were small, the only exception being the "liberation" of the individual voice. This was one of the signs of the emergence of the gig mindset, as discussed earlier. The low levels of the other points become a counterweight, limiting reachability and thereby resilience. They end up maintaining a traditional mindset and limit the responsiveness and interactivity of a gig-mindset work culture.

## QUESTIONS TO ASK: REACHABILITY

You can see how your organization scores on reachability by answering the 10 questions on the checklist below.[6] The items listed are indicative, not exhaustive. They are intended to provide food for thought and practical leads on how to increase reachability.

❶ Does our digital work environment reach the entire workforce?

❷ Does everyone in our organization have access to the enterprise social network?

❸ Can people throughout our organization reach people they don't know personally, using criteria such as skills and expertise?

❹ Can people anywhere in the organization find information—even if they do not know the source?

❺ Can customer-facing people reach the information and experts they need when serving clients?

❻ Can individuals from anywhere in the organization express themselves openly and directly using tools such as blogs, wikis, and Twitter-like tools?

❼ Do people and teams work out loud, making their work visible to people outside the project team before it is finished?

❽ Are customers included in our online communities?

❾ Do we have initiatives such as enterprise jams or crowdsourcing (and including frontline people) to solve problems and generate new ideas?

❿ Do we have participatory leadership whereby people are encouraged to give input to business goals, and to challenge ideas and work practices?

As you answer the questions, you may be thinking about gig-mindset behaviors versus traditional behaviors and how the former thrive or are stifled depending on the organizational work culture and technologies available. In Step 2 of the "Navigating Polarities" section in Part 6, "Defining a Perpetual Balance" (page 136), you will find a description of organizational work cultures—gig versus traditional—that are relevant to reachability as discussed here.

## How the gig mindset builds resilience

The table below summarizes the correlations between requirements for resilience and the gig-mindset behaviors and traits that reinforce it. The numbers refer to the list in Appendix A1.

| RESILIENCE CHARACTERISTICS | GIG-MINDSET BEHAVIORS/TRAITS |
|---|---|
| Reverse leadership | Prefers out-of-the-box thinking and test-and-learn approaches. (1) |
| | Often takes responsibility for initiating or advancing a project without guidance, and assumes responsibility for decisions. (4) |
| | Often challenges the status quo, including business and work practices. (5) |
| Accountable decentralization | Prefers out-of-the-box thinking and test-and-learn approaches. (1) |
| | Looks for opportunities to work with different types of people in different parts of the organization. Comfortable with responsibilities defined by skills rather than by roles and hierarchy. (2) |

| RESILIENCE CHARACTERISTICS | GIG-MINDSET BEHAVIORS/TRAITS |
|---|---|
| Fast learning | Comfortable with opening up early, working out loud, and receiving feedback from outside the project team as the project advances. (3)<br><br>Highly aware of what is happening outside the organization that can contribute to their work. Follows what's new in the social, economic, and technology worlds. (6)<br><br>Networks professionally, building relationships internally and externally. Seeks interactions with others to learn and share. (7) |
| Improvisation | Often takes responsibility for initiating or advancing a project without guidance, and assumes responsibility for decisions. (4) |
| Work-life balance | Growth path and personal brand are important. Feels primarily responsible for learning and increasing knowledge and marketable skills. (8) |

A gig mindset can make a business-critical difference and play, in the long run, a vital role in helping the organization survive and succeed. It is not a question of talking about a gig mindset. It must be lived. And it must start at the top. It must flow top-down, bottom-up, and horizontally across the organization. For this to happen, people who have been held back for years by a work culture based on a traditional mindset need to be awakened to the real-life benefits of a new way of interacting and working.

In Part 4, "Opening Minds and Organizations," we explore five ways to open minds and create the means for building a gig mindset and thereby more resilient organizations.

## CASE STUDY: #ILoveLearning at Air Liquide

Air Liquide is an international company with a presence in 80 countries. Founded in 1902, it has a long tradition of innovation. With sixty-seven thousand employees worldwide, it specializes in gases, technologies, and services for industry and the health sector.

### Self-learning and a virtual campus: A proactive initiative ready to go when needed

Gig mindsetters feel responsible, as individuals, for their own learning by increasing their knowledge and acquiring new skills. Organizations that are proactive in making learning opportunities available to people and giving them control over what they learn, and how, are likely to keep gig mindsetters motivated to do their best work for the organization.

Air Liquide is an example of a global company that was well advanced in the self-learning domain when a need emerged overnight—the Covid-19 pandemic. Thanks to several years of earlier work, the Air Liquide University was ready to meet people's needs when the crisis hit.

It was not starting from scratch. Air Liquide has a history of global initiatives geared toward empowering people, and facilitating interactions and collaboration. My research on Air Liquide since 2014 highlights the company's focus on people over tools. A strong focus on people helps organizations be resilient when faced with unanticipated and unplanned-for situations. The Air Liquide University took a major step in putting people first by developing a self-learning program for employees.

### #ILOVELEARNING, SELF-LEARNING PLAYLISTS

The self-learning program was launched in 2019 and branded as #ILoveLearning "Self-Learning for Everyone." It consists of a collection of digital resources available on-demand to all employees, designed to help strengthen their leadership, business, and soft skills. The collection includes e-learnings, microlearnings, "Executive Stories" (recorded by Air Liquide execs), digital magazines, articles, and videos, all of which are free and available to employees through self-registration. The self-learning resources are curated by the Air Liquide University with support from the business and global HR teams. They are then organized by topic into playlists, an appealing approach for people used to streaming music and movies. #ILoveLearning has grown quickly, with a new playlist featured each month in the #ILoveLearning newsletter.

When the 2020 Covid-19 pandemic started, the Air Liquide University met the challenge head-on. In February 2020, they launched the "Managing Virtual Teams" playlist, originally created to support the teams in Asia in response to the novel coronavirus. Shortly after, as the virus spread, they created a second playlist called "Working Remotely," translating it into seven languages. Other playlists are "How People Innovate," "Well-Being and Work-Life Balance," "Leading Transformation," and "Continuous Improvement."

## ADVICE FOR DEVELOPING A SELF-LEARNING INITIATIVE

Asked what advice they would give to other organizations interested in building a self-learning resource, the Air Liquide team reinforced the organization's relentless focus on people:

- Marketing of self-learning content is essential. People will not use the content if they do not know it exists.

- Communicate, communicate, and communicate again.

- Good user experience keeps learners coming.

  > Content should be curated by L&D and business teams to ensure quality and relevance.

  > Organize content into themes.

  > For translations to work, the entire learning experience must be translated.

- Experiment with strategies to increase utilization, ideally with a pilot group first.

- When scaling up and increasing audience size, be aware that there is a higher risk and you therefore need more checks and signoffs before launching new content.

- Ask for feedback, and strive for continuous improvement.

### VIRTUAL CAMPUS, A NEW EXPERIENCE IN LEARNING

As the coronavirus spread, many of the Air Liquide University face-to-face programs were canceled or postponed; they decided to create an opportunity out of this crisis and to "bounce back" with a new offer, "ALU Virtual Campus." Virtual Campus, a two-month learning event, took place from March 15 to June 15, 2020. The goal as stated by the Air Liquide team was to build a "mindset of being fit and ready to start when we are out of this health crisis." There were four content streams: Sales & Marketing, Management & Leadership, Innovation, and Operational Excellence.

The #ILoveLearning playlists were a key feature of Virtual Campus, with eleven thousand connections from three thousand learners. This was twice the utilization compared with previous periods. In addition, Air Liquide University launched two virtual learning offers during Virtual Campus: open webinars (available to all employees) and virtual by-invitation programs (for which people needed to go through their manager or HR contact), with content such as "Rapid Resilience: What Strategies Lead to Success?," "Virtual Facilitation," "Introduction to Knowledge Management," "Maximizing Team Performance," "Communicating with Impact," and "Full Engagement—Managing Your Energy." The webinars and programs included virtual classrooms and serious games.

The Virtual Campus was a big success, with over thirteen thousand log-ins from 3,600 participants from over 69 countries. They took part in 144 online learning sessions: 52 internally facilitated sessions and 92 externally facilitated sessions. This was achieved thanks to the contributions of over a hundred Air Liquide managers, executives, and external partners who shared their knowledge and experience with eager learners from around the world.

## GIVING PEOPLE LEARNING AUTONOMY

Both the ongoing #ILoveLearning self-learning and Virtual Campus event gave people at Air Liquide the opportunity to take charge of their individual development. Gig mindsetters strongly believe that their growth path and personal brand are important, and that they are the ones primarily responsible for learning and increasing their knowledge and marketable skills. This is exactly what Air Liquide has enabled people to achieve.

Interviews and information from Edith Lemieux, head of Air Liquide University and HR Transformation Projects, and David Ehlig, in charge of digital projects and communities for Air Liquide University.

# Part 4
## Opening Minds and Organizations

**Building a gig mindset** is both an individual challenge and an organizational challenge. You need to open minds. You need to open organizations. This means reducing old barriers and transforming ingrained ways of working that have existed for decades. I call approaches that can accomplish this "openers" because each contributes to opening individuals and organizations to the gig mindset. Openers are the first step, an essential one. They are:

- Reverse leadership

- Accountable decentralization

- Fast learning

- Improvisation

- Work-life balance

# Reverse leadership

IN BRIEF: Resilience is strengthened in organizations where it is recognized that leadership exists at all levels, in all parts. Leaders are people who exert influence that brings about change. Hierarchy has little to do with leadership. Gig mindsetters are often invisible leaders through their own behaviors that influence others.

Senior leaders need to have the courage to say "I don't know. What do you think?" and then listen to the answers. Management, at all levels, must encourage dissent and open disagreements. People need to feel free to challenge business and work practices, dare to question the status quo, and propose new ways of working.

The diversity of thought and ideas that result from this attitude in management enable the organization to be better prepared when a crisis happens. When unexpected events occur, the old ways of reacting may not be effective, and new ideas need to have already been heard.

Practicing invisible management is key to reverse leadership. It means that project leaders and managers give visible recognition to team members for their accomplishments. They remain in the background and do not take the credit themselves.

Gig mindsetters trust that their leaders will let them carry on their work and assume responsibility for the outcome. The fourth gig-mindset behavior, autonomy, illustrates this: "I often take responsibility for initiating or advancing a project without guidance, and assume responsibility for decisions" (see page 134).

A senior HR person working in the financial sector in Canada explained how leaders need to feel like partners with the employees:

> The whole idea of a gig mindset absolutely has to be modeled from the top. So, you need leaders who are comfortable working with or leading people who know more than they do, and putting themselves in a position of being partners as opposed to the boss who says, "I know everything, do what I say."

For a partnership to work well, there needs to be mutual respect and trust. In 1999, management consultant Jon Husband defined the seminal term "wirearchy" as "a dynamic, two-way flow of power and authority, based on knowledge, trust, credibility and a focus on results, enabled by interconnected people and technology."[1] He says leaders must "be prepared to listen deeply, be responsible, be accountable and be transparent." It sounds obvious but reverses the traditional idea of what many people think leaders should do— make decisions and lead the company to reach their goals. The key in Husband's definition are the words "two-way flow of power and authority." How simple yet how hard.

The traditional concept of leadership is alien to a gig-mindset culture, where the leader's role is turned on its head, reversed into a new dynamic of flows and interactions. Here is how a senior person working in the UK travel industry saw two approaches of senior managers:

You get two types of senior management. One is schooled in the hierarchical, top-down, "exploit existing knowledge, create efficiencies" operational type of organization. And, in that case, it's only top-down. That's worked very well through lots of organizations and continues to do so.

The other type is about value emerging from the ground up. And then you still need top-down management, but you need a different kind of top-down management. You need top-down management that recognizes that the value is coming from the ground up, and amplifies it rather suppressing it.

It's an excellent analysis. This is one reason I defined leadership in my research about the organization in the digital age as "the capability to influence and bring about change from any place and any level in the organization."[2] Leaders themselves must enact the principles of reverse leadership, rather than using their hierarchical positions to influence others.

## I DON'T KNOW: WISE IGNORANCE

Leaders need to live attitudes of wise ignorance, learning to say "I don't know," inviting questions, discussion, and debate among people. They need to embrace uncertainty and ambiguity, knowing that no one has all the answers. They must be able to admit they do not know everything. This sounds obvious, but it is not. Insecure or complacent leaders, working as they always have in the past, often feel an automatic need to display their knowledge and ability to make the right decisions. Strong leaders, on the other hand, create environments where people feel it is safe to step up and propose new ideas. Such leaders are rare.

A manager at a Canadian financial company spoke about how a leader with a gig mindset is more comfortable eliciting a variety of opinions and feedback:

> You need people who can manage people who are creative, who have very different perspectives. It can be far more challenging for a manager to say to people, "Okay, so here's this idea, what are all the things that could go wrong? What's your perspective?" That can be very difficult to manage. I get the sense that a gig-mindset manager is far more accepting of diversity of thought, and willing to see out the opinions of others, than is a traditional manager.

In my 2016 research survey on organizations in the digital age, three hundred managers in 27 countries were asked if they agreed or disagreed with this statement: "People in your organization feel free to provide input and challenge ideas, including business models and work practices." Only 40 percent agreed or strongly agreed. So, it seems that most people do not feel encouraged to question, to contradict, to express diverse views. Management has not created a work environment in which it is safe to challenge the way things are done.

## A SPIRIT OF CONTRADICTION AND DIVERSITY OF THOUGHT

Questioning is a natural part of reverse leadership, but it can happen only in organizations where leaders seek out diverse opinions and in no way feel threatened by disagreements. In fact, they encourage the gig-mindset behavior of the person who says, "I often challenge the status quo, including business and work practices."

Organizational theorist Karl E. Weick emphasizes how contradiction can be a powerful way to prepare for uncertainty. He discusses how a "spirit of contradiction"[3] is more productive than a "spirit of accord" because it brings out a range of ideas that are more helpful when dealing with the unexpected than is a polite conversation where everyone is in agreement.[4]

Consensus, once considered a noble goal to achieve before making a decision, is not effective in a volatile environment. Trying to build consensus actually decreases resilience because it means there will be a limited number of opinions and options to consider when a crisis hits and decisions need to be made quickly.

In addition, as we live a period of permanent uncertainty, today's consensus will likely be wrong tomorrow.

## INVISIBLE MANAGEMENT

Managers who enable their teams, who stay in the background, who give visible credit to their teams rather than seeking out the spotlight themselves, are a rare species. Why? Because their own professional image may be weakened. This is hard to do in work environments where promotions, raises, and personal reputation are based on visible accomplishments rather than on developing and empowering teams.

In a reverse leadership perspective, however, invisible management enhances one's professional image. Managers and their teams co-build an identity and share accountability. These managers understand that their role is to smooth the path, encouraging and enabling their teams to achieve results. A high-level manager in a UK-based healthcare organization told me about the risks of invisible management if your own superiors do not understand it:

In a hierarchical, top-down company, although nobody admits it out loud, you actually have to take credit for things your team does. You have to be seen to be the influential one. If I gave lots of credit to other people for the good things that happened, which I did, it looked to the very hierarchical manager that I wasn't doing anything. And in a way, I wasn't doing anything. But, in fact, everything I was doing was being done in the background. It was behind the scenes.

I was creating an environment in which people felt trusted and supported, psychologically safe, so that they would collaborate and experiment. And in doing those things, we would see value emerge from their interactions. But a hierarchical manager just doesn't recognize that at all.

As I'm building the context for my team, what I'm doing is giving them the room where they can find their own identity. And I'm giving them a narrative where we can build an identity together. And that identity is about doing innovative things, adding value to our colleagues.

I discussed middle management with Thomas Vander Wal, head of Strategy and Planning for DevSecOps and Collaborative Services in a large US-based organization. We talked about how many people think middle managers just get in the way, add no real value, and should be eliminated from organizations. His view was that a good middle manager plays three essential roles: financial, protective, and connecting:

Middle manager roles have changed and are there to clear the way for their people to do great work as well as provide what is needed to do a great job. Financing is key to the role, as is political cover. They also work as connectors in the network to bring insights from others to the team as well as skills that are needed. A team may have gaps in their network, and it is common for the middle manager to help find people to close those gaps.

Indrajit Gupta, the India-based analyst and editor, spoke with me about the importance of middle management in projects that risk pushing the boundaries, which is what gig mindsetters often do when they kick off new initiatives:

> From a practical viewpoint, when you have a challenging, innovative project, management needs to provide the necessary "air cover," such as resources and governance. Otherwise it risks failing because it is too new.

When things go wrong, the invisible manager becomes visible. When a project goes off track or is criticized by others in the organization, the team will probably need support. This is when the manager steps out of the shadows to take ownership and accountability, as well as to serve as a shield for the team.

Smoothing the path, providing "air cover," building an identity with teams while remaining in the background much of the time—this is the role of the essential, invisible manager.

These reverse leadership traits are rare. Fortunately, there are ways to enthuse people in their work and overcome the lack of engagement so many studies and surveys have revealed over the years.[5] You will see some ideas in the questions below.

### QUESTIONS TO ASK: REVERSE LEADERSHIP

Reverse leadership is a question of how leaders act, but also— and primarily—how people in the organization feel and act.

❶ Is our management comfortable when failures and problems are reported, so that people do not hesitate to escalate issues when necessary?

❷ Are people regularly encouraged to give input to business goals and plans?

❸ Do people feel free to challenge business models and work practices, to question the status quo, and to propose new ways of working?

❹ Do leaders seek and give feedback? Is it relatively easy to get a new idea to someone at the senior executive level?

❺ Do we have systems for getting input from the edges, such as from our customer-facing colleagues?

## Accountable decentralization

IN BRIEF: Resilience depends on decentralization. When decision-making, knowledge, and power are located in a single place, the organization is slow and fragile. Gig mindsetters are comfortable taking initiatives and responsibility without waiting for official approval and are therefore ready to act quickly when needed.

For decentralization to be authentic and to work in practice, the organization needs to have a limited number of high-level fundamental principles. People are then free to build initiatives, create projects, carry out actions, and experiment within this light framework.

People at the edges of the organization need to be listened to and trusted. It is they who are in close contact with customers and the external world. They scan the horizon, seeing things that management and central teams do not notice.

Unknown experts in the organization, often on the edges, may have better approaches to problems, based on their real-life experience, than do the official experts as defined by HR and as suggested by their hierarchical position. True expertise shows itself through what people do, not what they say, nor what is written on their diplomas.

### FREEDOM WITHIN A FRAMEWORK

Resilience requires that people in different parts of the organization are able to make decisions when necessary. Reliance on a single point or a single level means that decisions will be slow, potentially bottlenecks, because they can be made by only one person, who is not always the most knowledgeable about the issue.

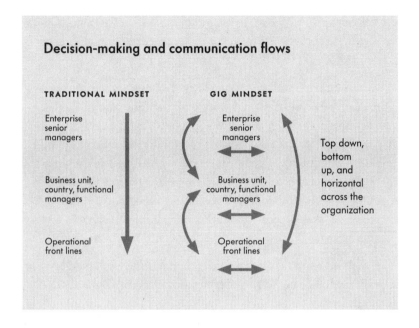

Fundamental strategic principles are the nonnegotiable pillars upon which initiatives, projects actions, and experimentation are based. They are the enablers of decentralized decision-making. They should be limited in number—between three and seven, ideally— and should apply across the whole organization. They free people throughout the organization to take initiatives, react when the unexpected occurs, and in general decide how they will work. Freedom within a framework liberates, stabilizes, and strengthens resilience. It provides a foundation for the gig mindset.[6]

The trick is to define the framework collaboratively with key players and to focus on what is essential. The process of definition will take longer, but when people are asked for their input and are involved in decision-making early on, you are more likely to secure their buy-in and active application. The support they will have within their own decentralized spheres of influence brings local credibility, which is essential for organization-wide principles. The "not made here" objection is eliminated.

A manager in a global healthcare company spoke about how an agreed-upon framework makes it easier to decide which processes are mandatory and which can be experimented with:

> We should not be saying, "What are the key things that we need to have processes for?" Instead, we should be saying, "What are the things that we absolutely must not deviate from?" Another way to get at what is essential is to ask, "What are the things where it doesn't really matter quite how we do it?" We can then allow people to get on and do what they are doing, as long as it's not illegal, in contradiction of the call of practice, dishonorable, or likely to cause deception or embarrassment. This way of thinking makes it possible to experiment within a framework.

A real estate construction manager in Nigeria explained how he sees the need for a gig mindsetter to work from standards that serve as a foundation:

> I work with a property development company and, from my experience, every project conforms to standards of construction and engineering that are established by professional bodies. But the point is this: established standards governing every job serve as a foundation for a person with a gig mindset to be at their best.

Another example comes from a global organization in the luxury sector headquartered in Paris. The individual brands were much stronger than the global company brand. I had been called in to work with the project steering group, made up of members from each brand and HQ. They were working on a global internal digital work platform and struggling with how the global HQ people wanted to define the digital strategy and how individual brand teams wanted to, with different brands preferring different approaches. We had at least five radically different ideas in the room. So, I guided the project steering team through an exercise through which they identified key principles. On the basis of these principles, individual brands could define their digital workplaces freely. After much work, they settled on three they felt reflected their shared values:

*The digital workplace, whatever the brand or country, should:*

• *Strengthen the links among us.*

• *Enable employees to make (good) decisions and take responsibility.*

• *Simplify everyday work and life.*

Other than following these principles, each brand team was free to design their own space within the global digital workplace. These principles are simple, logical, and easy to agree with on the surface. But they act as boundaries when people attempt, deliberately or inadvertently, to gain control or political dominance. In a subsequent work session, the strongest brand team had decided to keep their current intranet rather than join the group digital workplace, and as a compromise, just add a link between the two. It looked like the group project was falling apart. After much discussion, the strong-brand team agreed this was in conflict with the first principle: strengthen the links among us. They gave in, and the global project, which had risked failing, remained intact.

This is a good example of the strategic importance of agreeing on shared fundamental principles and writing them up in a short, cosigned manifesto. Using the three agreed-upon principles as a starting point made the project resilient. It did not collapse at the first sign of dissent. The brand teams had freedom, but only within the boundaries of the principles. Pre-agreement is the key. When a subsequent decision or action deviates from one of the principles, you simply ask whether people still agree with that principle. If they do, they need to adjust their actions. If they don't, the group is faced with the dilemma of whether to remove or modify the principle, or to somehow find a way to bring the offending party to agreement. Otherwise, the fundamental principles are weakened and will be of little help in future situations when difficult decisions need to be made.

## QUESTIONS TO ASK: DEFINING FUNDAMENTAL PRINCIPLES

If you are planning to define or review your fundamental principles, the following four criteria may be of help.

❶ Have we limited our fundamental principles to between three and seven, knowing that having too many dilutes the impact?

❷ Have we involved people at different levels and in different roles early on when defining our principles?

❸ Did we include operational management and people on the front lines?

❹ Did we include people from different business units or countries to participate actively in the discussion and decisions?

## STAY IN TOUCH WITH CONTEXT BY TRUSTING THE EDGES

Leaders need to have a feeling for what is changing, be aware of the risks they are running, and learn to think in fluid terms of decision-making, knowing there are no absolute right answers. They need to practice sense-making. Sense-making is not about finding the right answers. It is about being in touch with context, knowing as much as possible about what is happening around you.[7] Karl E. Weick, management thinker and author, talks about needing to stay in touch with context. He explains that it is not a question of following rules in order to make decisions.

Staying in touch with context means being close to where the action happens. This requires connecting the edges of the organization to the center and bringing the reality of frontline work through the management filter bubble. How can high-level leaders in organizations, in their comfortable offices surrounded by peers in their comfortable offices, stay in touch with context? This is a major obstacle in large organizations and is one likely reason small organizations are so much more reactive and ultimately more resilient: the people at the top are, in most cases, also on the ground, working alongside everyone else, seeing what others see. They are not isolated in ivory towers, out of touch with the edges of the organization.

People on the edges are often customer-facing and see more of the external world than do people in the inner parts of the corporation. They are very much the organization's eyes and ears, picking up signs of disruption and changing needs faster and earlier than their more internal colleagues. They are, at the same time, unfortunately, the most distant from the decision-making center.[8]

Freedom to create and make decisions from the edges brings a high degree of reactivity and resilience. Gig mindsetters flourish in this context and influence those around them.

## EXPERTISE BY ACTION

In a crisis, who would you count on? The official expert as defined in the HR directory or the person who has demonstrated expertise and served as an example and who has shared real-life experiences with others?

Experts are not necessarily those listed as experts by the HR department, but rather those who demonstrate know-how in action and in interaction with others. Hierarchical leaders must trust the experts and incorporate their input when decisions need to be made in the flow of action. More credible expertise comes from people who are working out loud, answering questions on the enterprise social network, or sharing information openly as they work. They consciously or accidentally build strong personal brands as experts.

Weick makes a strong point that shows a shift in decision-making. He says that gradually more decisions will be made by experts than by people higher up who, based on rank, would have made them in the past.[9] Unfortunately, managers in many cases are still making decisions, even though they are not necessarily the best qualified to do so.

An example from a worker based in the UK demonstrates this unfortunate state of affairs:

We are not allowed to make independent decisions. Everything has to be agreed by the director, even though they have the least time available.

Another example from Switzerland:

I have never experienced encouragement to take an initiative. Bosses, as I know them, truly believe they know it all.

An experienced mid-career manager in Denmark described the dilemma of how to manage managers who ignore experts:

Some parts of local management insist on providing solutions to experts instead of [providing them with] open-ended problems to be solved. People find this discouraging, as the proposed solutions are unrealistic, too high level, or impossible to implement. How do you explain this to a manager in a friendly way?

The examples above are negative ones, cases where management does not recognize the expertise of others and attempts to remain in control. However, gig-mindset-oriented people who build up a reputation as an expert in their field, and who are fortunate enough to work in a context where senior management recognizes their expertise, can build a stimulating, satisfying work environment. For instance, a 33-year-old man discovered how to build his creative space as he advanced in skills. He had evolved from a traditional-mindset to a more gig-mindset way of thinking, and finally felt he could make his own decisions about his work:

I think what happens is, as you get older, you move from the more traditional mindset to this more independent mindset as you become an expert in your field. Your manager or your boss is actually unable to comprehend your work, and that's why they're hiring you—it's an angle that they cannot cover alone because they have a sort of general idea of what to expect from your work, but they don't know how you work. So, you become independent and can define the terms on which you work. Today, there are companies where there is a space for you to still have the security of a full-time job but with the decision-making autonomy you need.

### QUESTIONS TO ASK: DECENTRALIZED DECISION-MAKING

Decision-making in a gig-mindset work culture is a process that frees people from traditional decisions imposed from higher up. Answering the questions below is a simple way to assess how close your organization is to a gig-mindset work culture because the responses to these questions will be "no" or "rarely" in a traditional organization and "yes" or "nearly always" in an organization oriented toward a gig mindset. Of course, in large organizations, the answers can well be "sometimes" or "yes, in some parts of the organization."

❶ Do we link responsibility to accountability?

❷ Do we place control and decision-making at the lowest level of accountability?

❸ Do we practice consultative decision-making, where people are required to communicate with the people impacted by the result before making the final decision?

❹ In general, do people feel they can make important decisions in their area of responsibility without seeking permission from someone higher up?

## Fast learning

IN BRIEF: Fast learning is a result of connected people interacting, sharing information, and developing skills in the natural flow of work. It makes organizations more actively alert to what is happening around them, thereby increasing resilience. This awareness and sharing are part of the gig mindset.

Work groups and communities let people discover, share, and develop expertise and skills in an ongoing way. Traditional training is useful in specific cases and subjects, but today, building strong relationships based on trust, both internally and externally, is more effective for fast learning than is the classroom approach.

Working out loud by making work visible before it is finished brings visibility to projects and people. It sends a signal that you welcome input and involvement from others. Serendipity may bring unplanned, useful discoveries that enrich the project.

## CONTINUOUS AND CONNECTED, INTERNALLY AND EXTERNALLY

Learning well and learning fast is crucial today. It is more important than what we typically measure when we evaluate business success. Esko Kilpi, who studied the art of interaction, the design of digital work, and the science of social complexity, firmly believed that how well and fast you learn is more important than the quantitative output of your work.[10]

Learning starts with individuals and is built from their interactions with other individuals. Problem-solving happens faster through these interactions. This is part of the personal knowledge mastery model developed by Harold Jarche, which is based on *seek-sense-share*. People *seek* new knowledge in networks and connections with others. They cooperate, giving to each other with no expectation of direct reciprocation. In communities, they develop understandings, exchange ideas, challenge assumptions. Then in teams, they work, collaborate, and create value together, striving to make *sense* of what they have learned. What results from this work is then, in different ways, *shared* with the communities and networks.[11] Too often, internal networking is favored, and the value of external interactions is forgotten. But they are complementary and equally necessary.

It is too easy to refer back to what we have learned in the past, even though it will probably not be the best indication of what we need to do today and how we need to build resilience. Learning can liberate us from the past. A researcher and analyst working in health outcomes in the medical industry said:

Unless we think about learning and practicing new stuff when the crisis (or pressure) comes, we revert to what we did when first successful.

The speed of change means learning must be fast, continual, and integrated into how people work and how they interact with each other. The proportion of organizations in surveys between 2013 and 2016 that feel it is *easy for people to learn in the natural flow of work* has doubled over three years, but it is still barely over half. Despite this increase, only 15 percent of organizations are confident they will retain the knowledge and know-how of people when those people leave the organization.

Let me share a Twitter exchange I had in 2016 with Esko Kilpi that explains his understanding of the dependence of knowledge on people:[12]

Kilpi: The knowledge assets of an organization are the patterns of interaction between its members. Knowledge is destroyed when relationships are missing or are destroyed.

McConnell: Do you believe knowledge is destroyed when people leave an organization?

Kilpi: Yes, always.

"Patterns" is the critical word in Kilpi's phrase "patterns of interaction." Patterns are regular and recurring. That's why you need a systemic approach to facilitate patterns of interaction among people. Communities and networks are part of this system. People need to be connected in a natural way—through communities and networks—that cuts through hierarchies and across silos.

The 15 percent of organizations that expressed confidence that knowledge would not be lost when people left the organization have mechanisms in place at a much higher rate than do other organizations:[13]

- 60 percent have communities for innovation and codevelopment (versus 40 percent in the full survey population)

- 95 percent have communities of practice (versus 80 percent)
- 70 percent have communities of interest (versus 55 percent)
- 60 percent have a single enterprise social network rather than multiple social networks (versus 40 percent)

An additional indirectly related difference is that a larger proportion have senior management that is "open and participatory" versus being "command and control." The attitude of top leadership clearly influences how people work and, in this case, how knowledge is retained.

Gig-mindset-oriented people feel personal responsibility for learning and believe that their growth path and personal brands are important. They connect with others, inside and outside the organization, through networking, interacting, and sharing what they learn. (The full behavior table is in Appendix A1.)

Staying ahead of the curve, following trends carefully, is powerful when what's observed is shared with others. Information and learning that is not shared, discussed, and adapted to different contexts is likely to remain abstract or "frozen in time." It is therefore of little value overall. This is true for people as well as of organizations. Kilpi placed learning in today's context by explaining that it is not a question of first acquiring skills, then using them at work. Instead, it is figuring out how to solve a problem, then scaling the learning up through other people and technology.[14]

A woman in her early 30s who works in a relatively small startup of approximately a hundred people explained their approach to learning through asking questions:

The best information you can get is by just asking anyone in the room. Everyone's encouraged to talk to each other all the time and ask questions. That's how the company knows they're going to have someone good right from the beginning. If a new person comes in and they ask loads of questions all the time, it's a better sign than someone who says nothing because they're trying to pretend like they know what they're doing. The people who say, "Hey, do you have time for a coffee? Can we sit down? Can I find out what do you do? How does your job work?" Those are the ones who will work out.

I moved from a very corporate company to a tech startup and, unlike in my previous job, this time there were no handbooks, no training, nothing. It was just asking questions, interacting with others, all the time.

A manager at a major Canadian bank explained why the company is ready to finance much of their people's learning, and how they expect people to share with others.

We are extremely supportive of learning and development, and that's one area on our employee opinion survey that we do really, really well. Employees appreciate that. Pretty much any learning that they want to do, we will support them, and we will help them find courses and so on, but we expect them to take the initiative. We don't go running after them to say, "Let's sit down and do your development plan." That's something that they have to take the initiative on.

We support people who want to go to conferences or courses. One thing we like to see is, if somebody does go to a conference, that they bring the learning back and share it with their team.

I remember one of our board members, a few years ago when we were talking about investing in training and learning development, and somebody said, "Well, what if we invest in all of this and they leave?" their response was "Well, what if we don't invest and they stay?"

The anecdote that closes the quote makes perfect sense. The perspective has been attributed to many people over the years, which goes to show how relevant it is. It has been credited to American business magnate Henry Ford, among others. It has been written up in various places as an imaginary conversation between a CFO and a CEO and used to support the need for training. My favorite use of it is by Richard Branson, who in 2014 took it one step further when he said: "Train people well enough so they can leave, treat them well enough so they don't want to."

## OPENNESS AND WORKING OUT LOUD

In 2010, Bryce Williams, collaboration specialist at a large US-based company, came up with a clear definition: Working out loud = Observable work + Narrating your work.[15] How does that relate to resilience? Working out loud protects you from unexpected obstacles, surprises you did not foresee. It is likely that others outside the immediate team will have input on a project, even when it is negative, and this can be beneficial in the long run. Others in the organization who are not directly involved may have valuable information, ideas, or contacts that will enrich the outcome. Working out loud became a "thing" in 2009 and has been since developed and used as a model by advisers and consultants.[16]

People who work with a traditional mindset sometimes believe that others will not be interested in a project until it is finished. However, usually it's that they do not want to run the risk of being criticized while the project is ongoing. They want the results to be "perfect" before showing anything to those outside the immediate team.

Working out loud can take place through different means of communication: a team or community space visible to all, a project blog open for all to read, or other digitally enabled techniques.

It is important to understand that working out loud is a practice, independent of technology. An example from NASA of working out loud long before digital work environments were the norm powerfully illustrates how it is a mindset, independent of technology.

Wernher von Braun, head of the Marshall Space Flight Center (MSFC, part of NASA), set up a system for working out loud half a century ago. Called Monday Notes, it's based on paper, pens, and a duplicating machine. It worked like this: every Monday morning, senior managers, lab directors, project managers, and other personnel sent a one-page note about the past week's progress and problems to von Braun.

Historian Roger Launius describes it this way: "Simplicity was the key: no form was required, one-page maximum length, only header was the date and the name of the contributor... von Braun encouraged his reportees to offer totally candid assessments, with no repercussions for unsolved problems, poor decisions, and the like." Von Braun read and commented on each note, congratulating success, asking questions, making suggestions, or giving critical feedback. The notes were then duplicated and shared with everyone involved.[17] The spirit of the gig mindset was at the heart of von Braun's open sharing in a test-and-learn context. Launius describes two benefits of the Monday Notes:

[They] made healthy conflict between organizations and persons at MSFC a realistic and useful management tool. The freedom (as well as the forum) to disagree was critical to the success of the organization. Disagreements that surfaced in the Monday Notes ensured that a variety of options and solutions were advocated. Evidence indicates that von Braun encouraged this type of conflict and was delighted that the notes were used to express it.

Encouraging disagreement and building a spirit of contradiction is one of the traits of a gig-mindset-oriented leader, as you will see in the next section. Unfortunately, this approach was later rendered bureaucratic—turned into official forms, becoming part of a traditional way of reporting—and no longer had the same impact.[18]

As with the NASA example from the 1960s, in which no technology other than a photocopier was used, a company headquartered in Latin America began to work out loud simply by using whiteboards:

One [piece of] feedback that I gave to a person was "I think you should use the whiteboard; that's something you have that you can use. There are so many whiteboards in this building, and you always just want to solve everything on the computer. Don't be afraid of writing stuff on the whiteboard and creating something new." It did not seem like such a big deal in that moment, but a year later she came back to me and said, "We just bought new whiteboards for all the areas, because we really want this to become a new practice. It helped us have better conversations in a simpler way... it breaks hierarchies in meetings... For most people, it was like nothing they had ever done before." So that was cool.

Openness increases the diversity of contributions and perspectives. Diversity saves time and is safer because risks are identified faster, as are actionable solutions. A regional government officer from Australia explained how she sees the value of open working in a context of diversity:

> People with different skill sets can give you a diverse perspective, such as "Have you thought about this, have you thought about that?" They flag risks, asking, "How would you deal with that?" Having people from different streams working together gives you a better outcome.

People assume that companies working in financial sectors need to keep their project work carefully under wraps, even inside their organization. In contrast to this, a manager in a Canadian financial company saw potential risks if you do not work openly:

> There are a lot of rules around privacy and reporting and client data protection and that sort of thing. So, somebody might come up with an idea... "Oh, we could do this. Our clients would really appreciate it," and if you've got the right people in the project team, whether it's legal or security, you'll get fast answers to questions. "Can we do this? How can we do this?"
>
> It may turn out you cannot do it, but you're more likely to find a different way to get what you want or at least find out early that you can't. If, on the other hand, you have people with a more traditional mindset who like to work on a project until it's fairly far

down the road before they tell anybody about it, it's hugely risky, because you could be spending tons of energy on something that could go nowhere.

## BRINGING NUANCE TO THE "IT'S CONFIDENTIAL" EXCUSE

A common excuse for not working openly is "It's confidential." Confidentiality is a valid reason for closing an information space when there is a risk of financial, competitive, reputational, or other damage if information is disclosed. It is helpful to discuss with the people involved which of these risks specifically seems potentially dangerous. Most closed workspaces do not represent true confidentiality issues. They represent power plays, as in *My information makes me powerful.* Or people feel reassured that their work cannot be criticized, since it is not seen. Either way, it's a sign that the work culture leans much closer to the traditional mindset than to the gig mindset. And it is likely that opportunities will be missed because of the limited exposure during the project work. There is little space for the serendipity factor, those unplanned and fortunate discoveries and ideas that happen in a spirit of openness.

## QUESTIONS TO ASK: OPENNESS ACROSS YOUR ORGANIZATION

Consider the questions below and think about raising these points with people around you and, in particular, management. If you are a manager, consider making these points part of the "normal" way of working.

❶ Do we work with senior leaders so that they learn to share more information?

❷ Do we recognize and raise the visibility of information sharers, especially leaders and managers who are active on enterprise social networks?

❸ Do we develop success stories around initiatives where information is shared openly, and promote them widely across the organization?

❹ Do we make it easy to share information? Do we make sure we do not over-formalize it?

❺ Do we encourage people to work out loud, sharing information on work walls, for example, where tasks and projects are made visible to anyone walking by?

❻ Do we have a guideline that all information sources in the organization are open by default (except highly confidential ones)?

## Improvisation

IN BRIEF: Improvisation means deciding in action when faced with an unexpected and unplanned-for event. It is deliberate and occurs without advance planning. Without the ability to improvise when necessary, an organization cannot be resilient. Gig mindsetters are highly aware of what is happening around them and are always ready to think and act "outside the box." They are able improvise when faced with the unexpected.

Improvisation is creating something new based on something that already exists. It is not creating something out of nothing. You use what you have at hand, but in a different way.

The work culture must be flexible, with a minimum number of layers and processes limited to only what is essential. Above all, there must be a willingness to accept experimentation and to learn from failures.

Improvisations range from small to major. Some will result in changes in how work takes place in the future. Others will prove to be short-lived, appropriate only for that particular unexpected event. The value of improvisation can be judged only after the fact.

## REAL TIME

Improvisation takes place when you are faced with an urgent, unexpected, and unplanned-for event and you try something new based on what you have available. It requires speed and happens in real time, with no time for reflection and planning.

There are three common myths about improvisation that we must clarify:

- Improvisation is an amateur having fun.
- Improvisation is innovation.
- Improvisation is an accidental mistake that turns out to be a great new product or service.

First, for most people inside organizations, the very word "improvisation" sounds like something you should not do. People who improvise are amateurs or fakers who do not know how to do things. This is a misunderstanding of the true sense of the word. In today's world of unexpected, unknown events and the need for speed, improvisation is a valuable skill.

A second misunderstanding is to confuse improvisation with innovation. Improvisation is real-time performance when faced with the unexpected. Innovation is the development of a new idea, product, or service. It is usually planned, developed after studies and interactions with users, or it may be triggered by someone's idea that then turns into an innovative project. An improvisation may well lead to an innovation, but only once it is determined to be repeatable and relevant in other situations.

Third, improvisation is not an accidental mistake that turns out to be a great idea for a new product or service. One famous example is the Post-it Note, which resulted from a failed attempt to create a super-strong adhesive for the aerospace industry: the weak, pressure-sensitive adhesive ended up on the sticky notes that we all use today. Other lucky accidents are the discovery of X-rays, quinine for curing malaria, Teflon, and superglue. And we may be able to put brandy on this list: by some accounts, it was accidentally discovered by a Dutch shipmaster who heated up wine to concentrate it for easier transport, intending to add water to it upon arrival. Needless to say, it was enjoyed in its concentrated state when the ship arrived![19]

By contrast, with improvisation, you consciously use what you have at hand, even if it is not perfect. Based on what is available, in material and people, you respond to an unexpected and unplanned-for event. Improvisation occurs when there is a need for speed. There is no time to organize a series of meetings and build a strategy.

An action must meet these four criteria to be considered an improvisation:

- It is intentional, not accidental.

- It is extemporaneous, not planned in advance.

- It happens simultaneously with the crisis or problem, not after stopping to think and plan.

- It is judged by hindsight, not by best practices and foresight.

## A CONDUCIVE CULTURE

Gig mindsetters are more likely to be able to improvise when faced with an unexpected event than are people with a traditional mindset. Several typical gig-mindset behaviors facilitate improvisation:

- The ability to experiment and learn through different approaches.

- Openness during project work.

- Being comfortable with taking responsibility.

- Working without needing hierarchical preapproval.

- The confidence to challenge the status quo and ask questions.

The capacity for improvisation must be grown inside the organization. It cannot be delivered by external consultants. It involves having a culture willing to rethink the way things are done. It requires challenging the status quo through actions and not just words. It requires accepting the need for speed. All this is part of the gig mindset.

Building an improvisation-friendly organization involves four key requirements. Each represents freeing people to operate faster and with confidence.

## 1. EXPERIMENTAL CULTURE

The organization's values and principles encourage action. Senior leaders promote experimentation, and the work culture tolerates errors when they become learning experiences. For example, people are encouraged to develop new ways of working on projects without needing permission. They are free to test new approaches to solving problems and encouraged to share the results with others.

One man I spoke to who worked at a company in the insurance industry shared that his company is facing new competitors and struggling to define their next steps. I asked if he felt free to experiment new ideas.

Him: Experimentation would not work in my company.

Me: Why not?

Him: Because management has a long memory, and no one wants to be remembered over the years as someone who failed in an experiment.

This organization lacks the first fundamental criteria for encouraging improvisation: willingness to learn from failure.

## 2. A DECLUTTERED, LOW-BUREAUCRACY WORK ENVIRONMENT

For most organizations, bureaucracy is their long-standing spinal cord. It is based on the division of labor according to roles, specified ways of making decisions and carrying out projects, and clear lines of authority, as reflected in the management structure. In some circumstances these constraints are necessary, but many times they result in blocking or slowing down experimentation, creativity, and new potentially positive initiatives.

Processes in most organizations are complex. For example, traditional processes for getting project budgets are complicated, requiring long-term thinking even when the needs over the next

12 months are not yet clear. A different approach, not yet widespread, is to work with agile budgets, where money is allocated step by step on the basis of multiple short-term checkpoints, rather than as a pre-set annual budget. This approach has a strong focus on observable outcomes.

3. MINIMAL STRUCTURE WITH "MENTAL" CONTROLS

Organizations have controls based on one or more of these criteria:

- Culture, vision, values
- Direct supervision
- Standardization and coordination mechanisms

If you want to encourage improvisation, you need a strong sense of culture, vision, and values. These are mental controls, as opposed to supervision or standardization. They enable people to take action fast, without going through levels of approval, as long as the action is in harmony with the organization's vision and values. Mental controls are indirect and need to be supported by clearly articulated goals and milestones. Management must live the vision and values through their own actions. The other levels of controls include constraints that are important in organizations with low levels of trust.[20]

4. SWIFT TRUST

Trust is usually built as people work together, but in today's global, virtual workplace, that is often impossible. "Swift trust" is not based on a history of interactions and shared experiences, as is the traditional concept of trust. It occurs when a group or team immediately assumes trust from the beginning and adjusts along the way as circumstances dictate.[21]

My research shows that digital maturity in organizations increases trust. Digital tools and platforms bring people closer together even when they do not know each other personally. In large organizations, this results in swift trust, where trust levels reach 70 to 80 percent in global management, in local management, and among other workers. These figures are under 40 percent for people in less digitally mature-work environments.

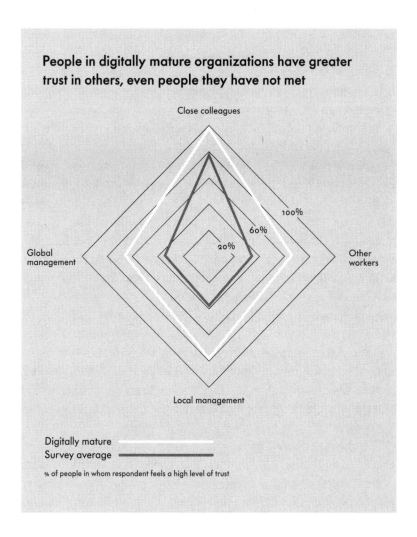

People in digitally mature organizations have greater trust in others, even people they have not met

Close colleagues

Global management

Other workers

Local management

Digitally mature
Survey average

% of people in whom respondent feels a high level of trust

The chart above shows responses to question "To what extent do people feel trust in their work environment and toward the following groups of people?"

## CONDITIONS FOR ORGANIZATIONAL IMPROVISATION

Organizational improvisation is a relatively new field in a topic that has been primarily covered from the perspectives of academic theories and jazz, a favorite metaphor for many researchers. The

2014 paper "Organizational Improvisation: A Consolidating Review and Framework" summarizes the situation by saying that organizational improvisation is becoming recognized as a relevant area of management research, but that there is still little research inside organizations.[22]

A notable exception, although over a decade ago, comes from Stephen A. Leybourne of Boston University, who conducted a four-year program of research looking at the cultural requirements to support the rise of improvisational working practices within the UK financial services sector. The study, published in 2009, was based on six retail lending institutions, including a major bank quoted on the stock market, building societies, and smaller retail lending organizations. We do not usually think of the highly regulated financial industry as a place to learn about improvisation, but the results are well worth reading and applicable to other industries.[23]

The research shows that the quality of improvisation is higher when the mental controls are focused on people, specifically customers, rather than on money. There is a correlation between a homogenous work culture with values expressed in terms of customers (*customer value, customer excellence, customer focus*) and the apparent effectiveness of improvisation, which was rated as "improving."

On the other hand, the apparent effectiveness of improvisation was rated as poor where there was a fragmented work culture with values expressed as *shareholder value, proactive product innovation*, and *growing profitable business*.

### IMPROVISATION IN A HYBRID GIG-TRADITIONAL ORGANIZATION

The case study at the end of Part 6, "Defining a Perpetual Balance," is entitled "Entrepreneurship in a Bimodal Work Culture." The company in question has a culture where improvisation is key to their success. They benefit from both the gig mindset and the traditional mindset, each supporting the other.

Quoting from the case:

[The front office people work] in a workplace of—in one word—
*impermanence.* There is constant movement. They have a
gig-mindset way of working by the very nature of their job.
Autonomy, awareness of the external world, initiatives, improvisation, and speed are strong dimensions of their work culture.
Other people in the company, known as the back office, working
in support functions such as HR or finance, have more traditional
methods, processes, and tools.

The case study includes a specific example of real-time improvisation that made a business difference during a crisis.

## KEEPING ONE EYE ON RISK

Leybourne believes employers are today more open to a gig mindset
in their employees than in the past. In a recent exchange, he talked
about the need to be conscious of risk:

Employers are changing their requirements when it comes to new
employees. They want self-reliant people with good interpersonal
skills who are able to think creatively and solve problems. That
sounds like a fledgling entrepreneur to me, and those skills, as
well as improvising effectively, sound like the way forward. I
see improvised work as simultaneous planning and execution—
deciding what to do and immediately doing it—but with one eye
on risk, in order to be able to "step back" to more solid ground if
things start to look hazardous.[24]

## IMPROVISATION IN EARLY STAGES OF A PANDEMIC

Improvisation, as you now know, is creating something new based
on what you have available, requires speed, and happens in real time.
There are two striking examples of improvisation from the beginning
of the Covid-19 pandemic in Europe and North America. Many initiatives occurred in the following months, but these two stand out for
their speed and timeliness.

Dimitri Syrkin-Nikolau, owner of Dimo's Pizza in Chicago,
observed the shortage of protective material in New York City

facilities and decided to make face shields in his pizza oven for his local area. As the BBC reported:

> "It seems unlikely that a pizza shop is going to be able to produce PPE, but the more I talked to people..." he recalls. "It seems far-fetched but it's not."
>
> After consulting with a couple of his engineer friends and pro-curing large sheets of acrylic, Syrkin-Nikolau and his staff have started making face shields for healthcare workers. The industrial pizza oven heats the acrylic up until it's soft enough to bend into the right shape, and then it is attached to a foam strip and straps.
>
> "It really is a very quick process," he says. "Whether it's sling-ing slices or slinging acrylic, it's similar principles."[25]

Although the equipment could not be used by hospitals because it was not approved by the US Centers for Disease Control and Preven-tion, nor by the Food and Drug Administration, they were used by organizations such as facilities for elderly homeless people, and by individual workers who chose to use them.

A second early improvisation initiative used diving masks from Decathlon, a sporting goods store, as respirators. This was born from a multidisciplinary project at the University of Alicante (UA), Artefactos. Javier Esclapés, UA engineering doctor and Artefactos coordinator, explained:

> We have adapted the Easybreath mask from company Decath-lon, creating an adaptor to insert one or two exchangeable HEPA particle filters (commercial and certified filters). This adaptor is manufactured with a material that makes the system totally air-tight, thus preventing external contamination.[26]

> Decathlon donated all their Easybreath masks to caregivers and hospitals.[27]

> Xavier Rivoire, head of external communications for Decathlon United... says the initiative started in the northern Italian region

of Lombardy, when a small 3D printing firm came to their offices to say that the Easybreath mask is the one product on the market that could most easily be adapted to use with ventilators.

"Decathlon Italy said yes to the firm, to donate masks to them but to also afford them use of the blueprint to make the product," he explained.

### QUESTIONS TO ASK: IMPROVISATION

The following is a nonexhaustive list of questions to ask yourself if you want to understand what factors may enhance people's abilities to improvise in your organization.

❶ Do you work with agile budgets, where money is allocated step by step on the basis of multiple short-term checkpoints, rather than as a preset annual budget?

❷ Are people encouraged to develop their own projects on company time without specific permission needed?

❸ Do you have a system whereby management can authorize people to develop new ideas based on formulating in advance the outcome they want to achieve, but without needing to specify method and detailed steps beforehand?

❹ Does your organization have flexible procedures for customer-facing people, letting them adapt based on context?

❺ Are there mechanisms for formalizing successful improvised work practices?

# Work-life balance

IN BRIEF: A resilient organization is made up of resilient people: motivated and energetic people who have a healthy balance between their work and personal lives. Getting the right balance has long been considered to be an individual challenge. For many years, people who burned out were considered to be weak or unable to control their schedules and pace of working. They themselves felt ashamed. This view is changing: long ignored by companies and people themselves, burnout is now recognized by the World Health Organization (WHO) as a syndrome usually caused by the work context. Gig mindsetters are in fact more likely to achieve the right balance because they have a sense of control over their work.

Longitudinal studies have shown the link between autonomy and personal resilience. My own gig-mindset research supports this observation. Even when people are working under stress, the more decision-making autonomy they have, the less likely they will suffer from burnout or have work-life balance problems.

Burnout is officially recognized in the WHO's International Classification of Diseases (ICD), 11th revision, as an occupational phenomenon and not a medical condition. The WHO definition calls it a syndrome, which is a collection of symptoms that indicate an undesirable condition. The WHO describes three dimensions of burnout:

- feelings of energy depletion or exhaustion;

- increased mental distance from one's job, or feelings of negativism or cynicism related to one's job; and

- reduced professional efficacy.[28]

Burnout was included in the previous version of the ICD but was defined then as a "state of vital exhaustion." The new definition is helpful in that it makes it possible to break down the condition and look at ways to avoid or deal with it. It also removes the stigma around the term by specifying that it is an occupational rather than a medical phenomenon.

A pair of researchers who reviewed 40 years of research on burn-out underline the importance it has in our world today. Linda V. Heinemann and Torsten Heinemann in their report say that the social and economic challenges we face today, and especially pressure in the workplace, mean that people at all levels, and in all industries, suffer from stress, fatigue, and exhaustion. Their research is especially interesting as it recognizes that burnout is not yet well understood. They say that research on this topic is vague and ambiguous, and the title of their paper—"Burnout Research: Emergence and Scientific Investigation of a Contested Diagnosis"—communicates their goal of clarifying the issues involved.[29]

Burnout is all around us, even though we may not be aware of it. People who feel burned out often also feel shame and hide their situation from colleagues. A digital-experience consultant shared her experience:

> I have burned out. Open discussion of healthy work habits and monitoring of danger signs might have helped. I am more aware of these signals in myself now.

As burnout receives more attention, it is gratifying to see people sharing their personal experiences. I was at a professional lunch in Paris in early 2020. Over cocktails, the subject of work stress came up. One person described his ongoing struggle with burnout, which had led his doctor to prescribe a three-month rest period away from work. He subsequently decided to leave the organization once he realized that his department head was not interested in improving team relations and that, if he went back, nothing would change. Another person shared the experience of a stress-induced heart attack, from which, fortunately, he was recovering. A third person told us about an official study, done by an independent third party, of the senior executives in his organization, a major global corporation. The study showed that one-third of the executives had suffered from or come

very close to burnout. What struck me is that these three examples—
of people I know personally—came from a group of only 20 people.

## THE SYSTEM, NOT YOU

It's not you. It's the system. Burnout is usually due to circumstances
within an organization and not to individual problems.

Eric Garton makes a strong case in his *Harvard Business Review*
article, "Employee Burnout Is a Problem with the Company, Not the
Person."[30] He places the responsibility squarely with the organization and management, identifying three causes of burnout:

- Excessive collaboration, which comes from having too many decision-
  makers and too many online and face-to-face meetings

- Weak time management and lack of teaching people how to better
  organize and prioritize their work

- Overloading highly talented people with too much work resulting
  from other people asking them often for information and help

According to the Mayo Clinic, a leading healthcare provider in the
US, burnout can result from lack of control, unclear job expectations,
dysfunctional workplace dynamics, and work-life imbalance where
your work takes up so much time and energy that you can no longer
focus on family and friends.

These factors are elements over which management has a good
amount of control. But, as we saw above, managers themselves are
victims of the burnout syndrome.[31]

Looking at the possible causes, we can easily see situations where
people do not have the time they need for reflection, thinking, or
absorbing ideas and information. A manager based in the US talked
about his need for time alone:

> I like a mixture of alone time and networking to gain ideas,
> connecting and then absorbing them to create new value or reart-
> iculate current ones in a broader perspective.

An employee in a high-tech company in the tourist industry believes most people can benefit from meditation. He said new
research in neuroscience is showing the value of reflection and
meditation:

> Quiet time, reflection, is very useful to process information. But
> maybe some people think "I don't have time for that." You know
> the Zen perspective? You should meditate for 20 minutes every
> day, unless you're really busy, in which case, you should medi-
> tate for an hour. It's that approach, I think, that brings value. And
> we're learning more about neuroscience around how that works.

The solution is to trust people, giving them autonomy. This brings us
straight to the fourth gig-mindset behavior, "I often take responsibility for initiating or advancing a project without guidance, and assume
responsibility for decisions." This is contrasted with the traditional
mindset of "I prefer working under guidance from my supervisor, with decision-making based on hierarchy." You will see later
in this section how control over work affects people's mental states.

For some people, however, the distinction between how they
live their work life and how they live their personal life is an artificial construct. I asked a building project supervisor in Nigeria who
participated in the research how he viewed the gig mindset and
work-life balance. His response:

> The person with a gig mindset applies the same energy to work
> and life. It's all the same. A person's approach to work is also their
> approach to life. Work is life and life is work. The behavioral pat-
> tern of any person affects the totality of the person's activities. A
> dedicated personality shows the same dedication in everything
> they do... at work, family life, study, sports life, and so on.

Many might think that gig mindsetters are subject to an unhealthy
work-life balance by being self-guided to achieve things that often
go against traditional organizational practice. After all, challenging

status quo business and work practices is risky. These people are potentially in high-stress situations because they often take responsibility for initiating or advancing a project without guidance, and assume responsibility for decisions. So, are they at risk?

## THE GIG MINDSET AND ALLEVIATING BURNOUT

Contrary to common opinion, the gig mindset alleviates burnout. My data dispel a common myth about the gig mindset, which is that the gig-mindset way of working risks triggering burnout because people are pushed or push themselves beyond reasonable limits. The reality is that gig mindsetters have a better work-life balance than do many of their fellow workers. This is because most people find themselves working under stress, but gig-mindset-oriented workers tend to feel in control, keeping a reasoned perspective even when the work is challenging.

My survey data show that people's perceptions of the challenge of maintaining a work-life balance depended in part on their individual gig-mindset scores. The survey question was:

> Do you think that people working with more of a gig mindset and attitude find it hard to keep a healthy work-life balance and potentially risk burnouts?

People with high gig-mindset scores broke into two segments: the "yes and" and the "yes but."

**The "yes and" group.** Some feel they run the risk of having an unhealthy work-life balance by spreading themselves too thin. They can't help going the extra mile, which can trigger stress and over-engagement at work. Plus, they need to be highly disciplined to do both their regular jobs and other initiatives they take on. Among the responses from my 2018 gig-mindset research:

- "Unfortunately, yes. If you have a more result-oriented focus (delivery focus), you get more tasks, as some of the more traditional-thinking employees don't run to catch the new and unexpected work."

- "Yes. Having a gig mindset is about discipline, or else you will end up running in circles, chasing elusive targets."

- "I deeply enjoy my work, and I find myself always thinking about it. Sometimes this means that I'm not as engaged at home as I should be."

- "Yes. As you are alone with your great ideas, you basically have to prove they work ... in addition to your daily job."

**The "yes but" group.** Others with high gig-mindset scores feel the gig mindset gives them extra energy, and they are therefore prepared to manage the challenge. Responses included:

- "Depends... maybe at times. A burning desire to connect, help, and pay it forward ends up keeping one busy in ways that aren't predictable."

- "If work drains you, you need to keep the boundaries strict, but if it nurtures and fulfills you, it is all just your life and you manage it that way."

- "No. Having this mindset, for me, leads to receiving more energy from the projects I am working on."

- "Now that you mention it, yes. But the alternative would be to toe the line, which may be even more difficult for these kinds of workers."

**The "no" group.** The segment of people with lower gig-mindset scores was the surprise. The people with a traditional mindset seemed to envy the strong-gig-mindset people.

They feel that a strong gig mindset brings a decreased risk of overload and burnout, because these people have more control over their lives and feel greater satisfaction with work than do those with a more traditional mindset. A strong gig mindset somehow gives "immunity" to work-life balance issues because the energy and engagement compensate for the potentially negative repercussions of being stretched too far. Among the responses:

- "Engagement in work is definitely higher, so this is when it becomes easier to ignore working hours and to accept to work more to achieve the goals of the initiatives."

- "Having a gig mindset is about passion to create, rather than about conformance to tradition. I presume that a certain tilted work-life balance would be acceptable to such a person."

- "For some, it can be the way to being happier at work. It can be also very positive for your work-life balance, because you can organize your life with less pressure."

- "People who embrace a gig-like attitude toward employment do so in order to improve their work-life balance."

- "Gig mindsetters… have a better healthy balance, since they feel more detached from the company and therefore able to draw limits when needed."

These responses from the 2018 gig-mindset research correspond to the results of a seven-year longitudinal study done by Indiana University's Kelley School of Business with a survey population of over two thousand people. The *Fast Company* article "Study Finds Work-Life Balance Could Be a Matter of Life and Death," by Jared Lindzon, provides an overview of the research. The study compares workers in stressful positions with high control with workers in equally stressful situations but with low control. Those with high control have healthier outcomes, even if their work is equally stressful.[32] This may seem obvious, but the degree of detail in the original study is thought-provoking and forces us to think about how the workplace can be improved, if only for the benefit of keeping employees healthy and not shortening their lives. Living a healthy work-life balance is possible through job motivation, facing challenges, and taking control. Now we have data that prove this.

Specific recommendations include not micromanaging people and letting them take greater control over setting goals and schedules. The research did not indicate that stress should be avoided at all costs. It did demonstrate that giving people the control and resources they need to manage their work can actually bring them satisfaction and increase their enjoyment of work, as it becomes a manageable challenge.

Just as a stressful job can be energizing, according to Erik Gonzalez-Mulé, the study's lead author, so can approaching projects with a gig mindset. Taking control of deadlines, pressures, and work approaches can bring satisfaction that, hopefully, management and colleagues can see and appreciate. This quote from a research participant based in Switzerland merits reflection:

> The gig mindset brings a sense of self-worth and place in the order of things.

### QUESTIONS TO ASK: WORK-LIFE BALANCE

Do you have a passion for your work? Do you identify so strongly with work that you do not have energy for your family and your personal life? If so, you'll probably need to get better control over your work by prioritizing what's most important and letting go of the rest. Here are questions to consider.

❶ Am I a high achiever (as are many gig mindsetters), and do I find myself getting asked to do more work than my colleagues? Do I sometimes fall into the ego trap and forget to find ways to involve others?

❷ Do I have a tendency to try to be everything to everyone and feel a need to help whenever I am asked? Do I need to learn to say no some of the time?

❸ Do I feel my workload is too high but hesitate to discuss it with my supervisor?

❹ Do I feel I have little or no control over my work? Do I need to discuss this with my colleagues and manager and find ways that will give me more autonomy?

### QUESTIONS TO ASK: COLLABORATION

Collaboration is usually a good way to work, but when it becomes excessive, it can accentuate burnout. You can set an example of ways to make collaboration effective and encourage others to follow your lead.

❶ Do I organize meetings and touch points only when absolutely necessary?

❷ Do I encourage holding stand-up meetings whenever possible to keep things moving fast?

❸ Do I use real-time meetings to make decisions, not to share information? Do I provide the necessary information in online spaces in advance of meetings and encourage others to do the same?

❹ Have I tried to find alternatives to email, such as online spaces where people can leave messages that can be read when needed?

A key guideline is to use asynchronous rather than synchronous communication. Messages in an online workspace or email that people can read at their convenience rather than real-time telephone or online calls requiring people to be "always on" are more respectful and efficient. It leaves people in control of when they access the information and limits the pressure and exhaustion of long real-time meetings, in person or virtual.

### FROM OPENING TO MOVING

In this section, we looked at five ways to open minds and organizations:

1. Reverse leadership
2. Accountable decentralization
3. Fast learning
4. Improvisation
5. Work-life balance

These starting points are essential for moving closer to a gig-mindset culture. In Part 5, "Investing in the Movers," we explore ways to recognize and keep gig mindsetters in the organization.

## CASE STUDY: Shift at Sanofi

Sanofi is a diversified global healthcare company, present in more than 170 countries and providing a range of healthcare solutions to individuals, as the focus is exclusively people. It consists of three core Global Business Units: Specialty Care, Vaccines, and General Medicines. Consumer Healthcare is a standalone business unit.

### Fast learning, a requirement for organizational survival in volatile times, combined with a gig mindset where people freely take the lead in their own learning

Sanofi has developed an original learning strategy based on three principles: Learn, Apply, Share. It starts with the person and finishes with the organization. It is a powerful way to blend the ambitions of gig-mindset-oriented people with the ambitions of the organization.

### BACKGROUND

Scientific and digital innovation go hand in hand. Machine learning, artificial intelligence, data visualization, and other advances are making life science companies redefine how they work. Digital transformation has been going on for well over 10 years but is now accelerating at high speed and creating a need for a workforce with advanced digital skills.

As Dany De Grave, senior director, Scientific and Digital Innovation at Sanofi, explains: "People do want to learn new tools, but there is too much competition for their time. Some can do that on their own time, but some need a helping hand to simplify the initial steps toward action and especially to translate new learning into application." He goes on to say that Sanofi is submerged in learning possibilities. You could spend all your time learning, but there is a difference between learning for yourself and making it useful for the business.

## LEARN, APPLY, SHARE

So, with the help of a few colleagues, De Grave developed the Shift at Sanofi initiative, the goal of which is to develop a large population of people at ease working with novel digital tools and approaches.

PreceptorShift, a key part of the Shift program, is the name Sanofi gave to this innovative approach to learning. It's a developmental opportunity for an employee to work on acquiring new digital skills and, importantly, to use them in their own environment.

The foundation is Learn, Apply, Share. People who want to kick off their own learning actions are asked to complete a formal but simple one-page document that poses six questions:

**What** will I learn? My target topic or skill.

**How** will I learn? Will I use online resources, or in-class training on- or off-site?

**Why** will I learn? I will acquire new knowledge or skills, but how will Sanofi benefit from my investment? How can what I learn be applied? The old question of "What's in it for me?" is complemented by "What's in it for Sanofi?"

**When** will I learn? I expect to focus on this specific topic between *this date* and *this date* and commit X percent of my time, on average.

**Where** will I learn? Will it be my usual work site, or another place?

**Who** will help me? Who will my mentor(s) be? Who will help me make this a success, for myself and for Sanofi?

Once the form is completed, the employee's manager emails it to the dedicated Shift email inbox, which implies approval.

De Grave emphasizes: "Because we put this on paper, it has become part of the job, there is an investment here, we want to see how it is used. It will be included in performance evaluations, because it's an activity like all others. It's not a sideline or an after-hours task."

The sharing part is very important, and people are encouraged to share their newly acquired learnings and selected outputs in the dedicated Yammer community and in local onsite communities as well. "The goal is to grow together in our learnings, so we don't need to reinvent the wheel."

## OPENING OPPORTUNITIES

PreceptorShift is a way to open opportunities for people inside Sanofi.

"When we need people with a specific digital skill, we can advertise that there is a project needing 10 people part time, and via PreceptorShift they can acquire the needed skills."

The program helps people learn basic tools such as Simpleshow, to make clips explaining something from their work, as well as helping people with more advanced tools. "There was a biostatistician studying machine learning at a university on his own time outside of his work at Sanofi. Our Shift team contacted him and discussed how we could help him make the next step in his career while staying at Sanofi. We offered to give him real data sets to work with, and thereby made his work valuable to Sanofi as well as serving as real-life material in his course. The result? He stepped into a new role at Sanofi rather than looking for a new job in a different company."

De Grave has had a long experience with gig-mindset-type projects. In 2014, he created Project M, an enterprise-wide initiative that let people set up a project, do something new, and be supported by the M-Connect platform for online sharing. There was no need for manager approval. There was no official budget. The only condition was that the new initiative did not interfere with the person's full-time job and departmental deliverables. This was fine for people who wanted to drive change in any way they could and were ready to go the extra mile, but it was not easy for everyone.

## DEEPER AND VISIBLY TRANSFORMATIVE

PreceptorShift has gone both deeper and higher. The one-page document and manager approval mean it is recognized as work, and something the company now expects to happen. There is a lot of communication and recognition in the Yammer communities, where people share what they are doing and ask questions. This helps develop working out loud, and people discover that communities can be a way to get quick answers to questions, because they are tapping into a large pool of people. Experts are popping up organically, through their actions, sharing and helping others via Q&As.

De Grave summarizes: "Overall we try to make it as easy as possible for people to develop themselves further toward a digital mindset while creating a collaborative environment which, like Project M in the past, has a part of serendipity to it. However, because it is more visible, it is easier for us to watch how it changes decisions people make, helps careers advance, and inspires others to take their own first steps."

Shift at Sanofi is an example of an organization that is deliberately cultivating a gig mindset inside the organization. It encourages and celebrates the gig-mindset behavior of networking and building relationships internally and externally, and actively seeking out interactions with other people from whom they can learn and to whom they can contribute.

Interview with Dany De Grave, senior director, Scientific and Digital Innovation. www.sanofi.com.

# Part 5
## Investing in the Movers

## Debunking myths

IN BRIEF: Organizations have long talked about investing in people. I use the term "movers" to reinforce the image of gig mind-setters and their natural drive to move their organization into the future. They strive to bring new ways of working that are adapted to today's world reality to their organization. They work to move the mindset of others to their way of thinking in order to achieve relevance, resilience, and success together. The terms "gig mind-setter" and "mover" are used interchangeably to underline the fundamental role they play in organizations.

Movers are essential to the future of organizations, so it is important to clarify some common myths.

Myth 1: **Movers create chaos** by encouraging uncontrollable flows of information, ideas, and opinions.

- *Reality*: Movers stabilize the organization. Their gig mindset helps increase the speed of learning through extensive interactions with other people across and outside the organization. They bring information and ideas into the organization that can be essential when there is a need to create something new or to improvise.

Myth 2: **Too many movers is risky** for the organization.

- *Reality*: It is highly risky for organizations to not have enough movers. This is because they need people who are able to take the unexpected into account, people who dare to go beyond proven and approved methods and to experiment. They need people who can make decisions and take initiatives, people who mobilize and advance projects without needing a detailed plan and instructions.

Myth 3: **It is safer for individuals not to be movers**, not to stand out, because you believe you can count on the system to support and guide you along your career.

- *Reality*: If you're not a mover, you risk being trapped in one-way dead-ends and missing out on internal opportunities because of lack of relevant skills and knowledge. You will likely have insufficient awareness of the external world and trends that could impact your work life and career.

The many valuable characteristics that gig mindsetters bring makes them crucial for organizations that wish to maintain relevancy and thrive in today's ever-shifting global context. We are beginning to recognize the value of gig mindsetters and are entering an era where they will be sought out as valuable players rather than considered as a threat to hierarchy. Organizations therefore need to create stimulating, motivating, and creative opportunities to attract and retain them.

If organizations fail to create such an environment, they risk ending up with a workforce with skills that are no longer relevant, and, worse still, losing top talent because their people move to more challenging employers or startups, where they can give full rein to the gig-mindset approach. The pressure is on, as top talent is sought out by startups and other organizations moving fast to gain competitive advantage.

In Part 1, "What Is the Gig Mindset?," I quote a manager of a global company in transport solutions who is based in Sweden; he explained that creating an organizational culture that embraces the gig mindset is important because it motivates and helps keep—and attract—the "best people." An employee in a hundred-person startup in the Netherlands has experienced this very result:

> We just got a new guy in our company. He's about 35 or so and used to work pretty high up at [name of globally famous brand company]. He resigned and came here. He's making much less money, he says, but the work is more interesting, and he's enjoying himself much more.

Gig mindsetters will be in greater demand as automation and AI (artificial intelligence), including machine learning, are used to carry out enterprise processes. A gig mindset cannot be replaced by AI. But people with gig mindsets can use AI to handle their routine duties and help them manage data, leaving them free to create and innovate.

Loss of top talent is a risk that traditional organizations run today. This trend of established organizations losing talent is confirmed by the BSI *Organizational Resilience Index Report 2019*, discussed in Part 3, "Building Proactive Resilience." Sustainability of organizations correlates to retaining talent, and companies are faced with higher turnover than in the past and low employee engagement.[1]

How can organizations recognize, keep, and benefit from gig mindsetters? A starting point is to rethink what the word "job" means.

## Rethinking what a job is

IN BRIEF: As seen earlier, gig mindsetters do not define jobs in the same way as do people with a traditional mindset. We've been using the word "job" for so long, it seems natural to us. Now is the time to rethink what we mean and whether it still applies, given the volatile times we live in.

"Job" is defined in both the *Merriam-Webster* and *Cambridge* dictionaries in a similar vein: the position a person holds or the regular work a person does to earn money. Other definitions are more mission- or goal-oriented: "a specific duty, role, or function," and "something that is your responsibility."[2]

The *Business Dictionary*'s detailed definition encompasses how organizations manage jobs:

> A group of homogeneous tasks related by similarity of functions. When performed by an employee in an exchange for pay, a job consists of duties, responsibilities, and tasks (performance elements) that are:
>
> (1) defined and specific, and
> (2) can be accomplished, quantified, measured, and rated.[3]

These definitions, especially the last one, lead us to conclude that jobs must be defined specifically enough that the duties, responsibilities, and tasks can be measured and rated, *assumedly by using standardized organizational systems.* Here we are moving into the territory of the traditional vision of a job.

This is indeed the starting point for many organizations. A job is a role with a title and level that fits into a box in the HR matrix. Examples are Assistant Manager, Head Buyer, Payroll Coordinator, Head Designer, Key Client Account Manager, and so on. Job titles that indicate the person's level within the organization reveal a work culture primarily based on hierarchy. You need to know the person's level before you interact with them.

You've likely heard people say "That's above my pay grade" when asked to make a decision or take an action. It's an excuse to not step up and assume responsibility. It's what I call "hierarchy speak" and is most often heard in organizations with rigid hierarchies and low autonomy for their people.

A precise role can block people more than enable them. An overly defined job is a limitation, not just for the individual but also for the organization. It will neither attract nor keep gig-mindset-oriented people because it is too restrictive. Jon Husband, who defined the wirearchy concept,[4] explained how we are still inside the boxes despite talking about thinking outside the box:

Today our charts, job descriptions, performance objectives, bonus schemes, all of this stuff that is effectively a straitjacket, it encircles people. KPIs [key performance indicators] and measures become constraints much more easily than they become enablers. Talking about experimentation and thinking outside the box is fine, but we need to realize that although the phrase has been around for 20 or 30 years, the boxes are still there.

The industry-recognized Gallup polls report that, depending on the year and the country, between 10 percent and 17 percent of employees are actively disengaged. The proportion who are simply disengaged reaches as high as 60 percent or even more. Only 15 percent are engaged or "highly involved in and enthusiastic about their work and workplace."[5] Taking these general results into account, the following definitions of "job" from the crowdsourced, sometimes controversial *Urban Dictionary* are less surprising. They may make you cringe, but most ring true in different ways:

"Means by which at least 30 percent of your life is stolen from you to enrich the owners of a company making useless shit that some other poor idiot in a job will buy." Voted up to position 1.

"A thing that takes up much of our lives and sends a message to everyone that life sucks." Voted up to position 6.[6]

Why not replace the concept of job with the concept of role, mission, or goal? By "goal," I do not mean job goals to be integrated into performance reviews and management by objectives methods. I mean overall strategic objectives. This approach would be meaningful for skills that can be integrated into a series of different projects, or that can play a role in spontaneous missions that come up ad hoc as circumstances and business environments change. Here are examples of phrases (not titles) that can be used on business cards and email signatures: collaborative experiences designer, sustainable business transformation, inclusion facilitator, networking coach.

This approach would help organizations become more resilient as disruptions occur around them. The people are identified by roles and expertise, and not visibly limited by management levels and HR boxes.

## Going beyond the cv

IN BRIEF: If you want gig mindsetters inside your organization, you need to attract them and keep them. For either of these to be possible, you need to recognize them when you see them. This is the trickiest part, because traditional techniques for interviewing and evaluating job candidates will not be effective. You need new approaches.

A research participant based in the Netherlands was adamant about what type of people their company sought out and the importance they placed on their attitudes during the recruitment process:

> In my company, they don't want people who come and are told what to do. They want people who come and have ideas and make suggestions. This needs to happen during the first interview. If it does not, the person usually goes no further.

However, these qualities are not at the top of the list for most HR recruiters, as illustrated by the chart below. In research I conducted in 2016 with approximately a hundred people from companies around the world, I proposed a multiple-choice list of criteria. Ninety-eight percent of survey participants said that new people were hired based on their knowledge and skills; 78 percent said they took into account the ability of the person to learn to adapt and evolve. Only 28 percent said a criterion for them was "the ability of the person to offer alternative opinions on key subjects (e.g., challenge assumptions, engage debate)."

Today, given our fast-changing times, the second criterion on the list is actually more important than the first one: the ability of the person to learn, adapt, and evolve. The most important is the

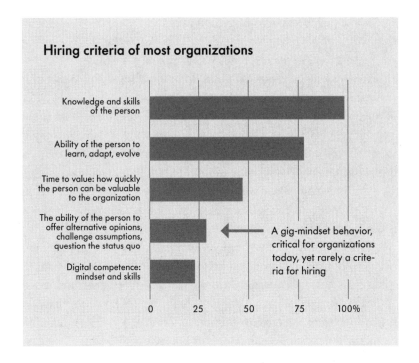

Hiring criteria of most organizations

next-to-the-last one: the ability to offer alternative opinions. This capacity can be more important than the knowledge and skills a person has upon entering the organization. It is an inherent part of reverse leadership discussed in Part 4, "Opening Minds and Organizations." Leaders need people around them who dare to challenge them and who engage in thought-provoking, sometimes controversial, discussions. Recruitment and evaluation processes need to identify people who have this ability, or, at best, eliminate the "yes" people. I am not saying that all workers in an organization need to continually challenge the status quo, offer alternative ways of working, and so on. However, when the context demands it, people need to be ready to do so, and leaders need to be ready to listen. In fact, as described in Part 4, the work culture needs to be one in which there is a spirit of contradiction, meaning that people are alert, observant, and able to interact and make suggestions whenever they feel the need.

So, during the hiring process, how do you identify people who have a questioning mind, are willing to challenge the status quo, are able to take initiatives and ready to assume responsibility?

Interviewers can look for signs during the interview itself that suggest the job candidate will potentially be at ease asking difficult questions. One HR recruiter told me that they are now more interested in people who ask a lot of challenging questions during their job interview than those who simply ask questions about the company's business model and ways of working.

A telling line of exploration, but one the interviewer often neglects, concerns the job candidate's business network. The point is not to invade privacy by examining the person's network but to simply find out if the person does networking outside specific job needs, and if so, how. Good questions to ask are "Do you feel you get value from your business network? What value do you get, and how?"

Subramanian S. Kalpathi, author of *The Millennials: Exploring the World of the Largest Living Generation*, explained what he thinks is important for companies to ask job candidates:

> One of the important questions for employers is how big the person's network is, digital network, social network, especially externally. Companies are looking for people who have significantly large networks, because those people are more aware of what's going on in the world.[7]

Some interviewers often look at the candidate's spare-time activities, as these can bring depth to the people who do them and value to the job. Smaller companies are more likely to appreciate that, especially those in a creative industry. However, I foresee this trend becoming more important in large legacy organizations as many of them make efforts to be more human, to live the values they preach. For example, a person who works for a not-for-profit in their spare time will likely bring its values to the workplace.

An interesting technique is to put the candidates on your shortlist into real-life situations, to get a sense of how they interact with others. A senior manager in a 140,000-employee global insurance company headquartered in Europe explained how his division evaluates job candidates:

> We invite people who interest us into a day-long work session, a real work session with our team. We want to see how they interact with the other people. That's very different from the past, when job candidates just got interviewed by an HR person and the manager and either got the job or didn't. This approach gives us a better sense of what they are like. It's good for the person as well—they get a feeling for the team dynamics and how our people work together. Of course, it makes some people nervous, but that's normal. We usually manage to make them feel at ease.

### QUESTIONS TO ASK: HIRING IN THE GIG-MINDSET AGE

The following questions offer ways to make the hiring process more meaningful for both you and the job candidate.

❶  Do we consider their mindset and adaptability as much as we do their experience and expertise?

❷  Do we engage with the job candidate in such a way that we can see if they are comfortable offering alternative opinions, challenging assumptions, and engaging in debate?

❸  Do we consider the extent of the person's professional network and whether they seek out interactions with others?

## Evaluating with care

IN BRIEF: Performance evaluations based on formal interviews between people and their managers are artificial and can be misleading to both parties. They do not shine a light on the outcome of people's work beyond limited quantifiable measurements.

You will get what you evaluate and not necessarily what you want. There are other techniques based on dialogue and feedback that will be beneficial all around.

## WHAT NOT TO EVALUATE

Harold Jarche, personal knowledge mastery expert, points out how the individual performance evaluation system can go wrong:

The individual performance measurement system misses a lot of value. Even though cooperation, doing the right thing, or being safe may be promoted, if the performance management system rewards people for acting individually, then they will continue to work that way.[8]

The following examples from research participants in Sweden, Australia, and the US respectively illustrate how many organizations practice a limiting traditional approach to performance evaluation— and that it is neither a national or cultural phenomenon, but occurs across countries and industries:

We are not rewarded to do things that were not in the plan.

We prioritize constraints over the benefits of change. There is no effort to develop change management skills. There's no flexibility in annual budgets. There is reward and promotion for those who maintain the status quo.

One of our worst actions is rewarding competitiveness. Hoarding information is often a result.

## EVALUATING THE INVISIBLE

If you work in a gig-mindset way, you face two challenges in performance evaluation that traditional-mindset-oriented people do not. The first is that you likely play changing roles in the organization as you join different teams on different projects. Your work may seem vague to management, who may wonder what it is you actually do and what value you bring to the organization. Much of your work may be invisible to them.

A senior manager with experience in several organizations over the years reflected on how this fluidity can have a negative impact on gig mindsetters when times are hard:

> If there's distance between you and the senior executives, the more nebulous it is what you do and how you're identified, the harder it is for them to get a good grip on it unless they have been a direct project sponsor and you have built your internal brand with them. You need to manage up, and lack of clear, consistent role definition is a handicap.
>
> If an organization is going through a period of contraction and looking to reduce headcount, they're looking to reallocate budget. Somebody whose role is not clearly defined and doesn't have an official job title could be in trouble, even if they've been adding value all the way along.

Gig mindsetters have roles that cut across the organization and across silos and which are not easy to understand. Their work is driven by a desire to improve something others may not see. This may seem vague to management until a "real" project is shaped. Recall the quote from Part 2, which highlights a crucial point in understanding why it is so difficult to evaluate the contribution of gig-mindset-oriented people:

> They often work undercover, in the gaps between official initiatives, bringing life to spaces in the organization where previously there was nothing. When the project takes shape and is sustainable, often someone else takes over because the organization prefers a visible project manager with a clear, understood profile.

This is similar to what happened in another organization when an innovative idea was so big and so critical to the future of the company that it needed to be managed at a very high level, far beyond that of the person who came up with the idea. One of the people involved described it this way:

> One person who recently left the company had been here for 10 years. He left to join a startup, because one of his ideas actually

became the biggest IT project in recent history in our organization. He was recognized as being one of the people who originated the project, but it was just too big for someone of his profile. The project involved changing the entire IT infrastructure of the group, so it had to be the CTO [chief technology officer] who took over. People did not wonder why it was the CTO and not the person who had proposed the idea. It was clear that the CTO should run it. For example, two hundred contractors had to be hired because we didn't have enough in-house skills and staff.

The person who had the original idea left because it had become too big and too much of a traditional project. He felt like he had trapped himself in this big standard mammoth project, and he just wanted to go and do something agile and different. But having been the father of that project, he couldn't really abandon it, so he left the company, because he couldn't just switch to another team. He decided to leave for a more creative and experimental environment.

The company lost an obviously innovative mind because they had no position within the current structure that could satisfy his creative, curious, and experimental mindset.

### WHAT TO EVALUATE

These are times when good talent will be lost, as in the case described above, unless senior management has clarity on the values brought by gig mindsetters.

A research participant from India talked about how innovation dies in people:

> When work is all about client deliverables and there are no rewards for ideation or problem-solving, we slowly kill the innovative side of people.

#### LOOK AT BEHAVIORS, NOT WORDS

The Competency Model developed by Merck KGaA, Darmstadt, Germany, is an inspirational yet pragmatic approach to evaluating people before hiring them and all along their career inside the organization.

As you saw in the case study at the end of Part 2, their model is more than an evaluation framework; it enables new methods of work, letting people personalize and apply behaviors to their context as individuals and as part of a teams and an organization.

## LET PEOPLE TAKE CHARGE

Another challenge is to go beyond traditional cookie-cutter job roles and find ways to let people's interests and skills emerge and develop into job roles. BlueShore Financial, in Canada, has an unusual feature built into its work culture. Called Velcro management, it gives freedom to people within a strategic framework, combining flexibility with purpose. You can read more about it later in the case study "Velcro Management in Action."

## SOCIALIZING PERFORMANCE MANAGEMENT

Socializing performance management is a promising, relatively new practice that reflects people's work and results. It is based on continuous dialogue and feedback where managers and employees establish and share goals with each other and track progress in real time, as opposed to the traditional one-shot annual exercise. Data from my research in 2014 show that 4 percent of organizations practiced social performance management, with another 24 percent doing so in some parts of the organization. Two years later, the numbers went up slightly, to 10 percent in the whole organization and 23 percent in some parts. However, this practice is not yet sufficiently tested with case studies over time to allow definitive conclusions to be drawn.

## QUESTIONS TO ASK: PERFORMANCE EVALUATION

The following questions offer ideas as to how to make performance evaluation more relevant, to people and to the organization.

❶ Do we practice dynamic performance evaluation based on regular communication and frequent assessments, project by project?

❷  Do we include peer feedback and bottom-up feedback all year long?

❸  Do incentives include team-based performance as
well as the individual perspective?

## Liberating talent

IN BRIEF: Gig mindsetters have a strong drive to learn, develop,
and control the direction of their careers. They attach high importance to their growth path and to increasing their knowledge
and skills. Unlike people with a traditional mindset, they do not
count on their manager or the HR department for guidance. They
may think in terms of a personal brand, the image others have
of them and how it is marketable, including inside their organization. There must be a means to give visibility to the people's skills,
knowledge, and ambitions in order to stimulate them to grow
within the organization. Otherwise, they are likely to leave.

The idea of a personal brand stimulates some people but puts others
off. It sounds conceited, as if you were selling yourself as a product.
The job-market reality is that you *are* in fact selling yourself, especially inside the organization, where changes happen as fast or faster
than in the external market.

I had a conversation years ago with the leadership of a large public transportation organization that was just starting an internal
social network. There was concern about the employees oversell-
ing themselves when describing their skills. After much discussion,
the head of HR made the point that, in the case of an internal job
market, any exaggeration of skills and knowledge would be quickly
noticed by colleagues and unlikely to be a lasting problem. The word
would spread fast. People who oversold themselves would not get
many "likes" and "recommends" on their profiles and contributions
to online conversations.

A big advantage to letting people actively look for new work and
new roles inside the organization is that it makes it more likely they

will stay with the organization. They may do this in the organizational social network, in the talent marketplace if that exists, or simply through their informal network of contacts. Whatever the approach, they will feel freer to grow and develop their skills without needing to change companies.

An experienced employee in a small startup in London explained how people can now evolve without leaving, assuming they have a gig mindset:

> Before, if you were doing a job, you would need to change company much more regularly, year on year, so that your role would evolve, you'd be paid more, and you'd find your job more interesting. But now I think people who have a gig mindset can stay in the same company and evolve their job into something that they want more without having to leave the company.

A manager in a European national health service expressed the same idea:

> I think every company tries to offer career paths, career growth, opportunities for movement within the company because they do want people to feel like they can move in the company without leaving the company.

A third example from one of the largest global financial services organizations in the world reflects the same strategy:

> During half-yearly assessments, it is made clear to us that we are responsible for our careers and should not wait for HR or our manager to offer us the next job.

## TALENT MARKETPLACES

Internal talent marketplaces give people more control over their work and how they want to evolve. Many companies do talent inventories based on predefined skills. They are usually managed by HR departments based on definitions, boxes, and levels in organizational charts. But internal talent marketplaces where people can sell themselves are much less common. Inventories meet an administrative need, whereas such marketplaces empower people. Workers define their profiles based on their skills and interests. This puts them in a position to have projects that are more satisfying to both themselves and the organization than they would if they were limited to what their official role involves. One worker in an organization with an internal talent marketplace explained a major advantage:

> Marketplaces encourage people to raise their hand and "opt in" for things that they are really interested in, either as a side project or through internal movement of talent.

However, most organizations do not have internal talent marketplaces. Data from the 2018 Gig Mindset Survey show that 50 percent of the very large participating organizations (over a hundred thousand workers) have them, probably because their size has made it a necessity. Only 20 to 25 percent of smaller organizations reported having internal talent marketplaces.

Not all internal marketplaces are successful. A good idea can be stuck in the past because of how it is implemented. In the next example, it's clear that it was the way the internal marketplace was implemented that made it feel like a company-owned rather than an employee-owned initiative:

> In one division of the company, they were starting to talk about a marketplace for people. But then they got stuck on the idea that the managers ... had to agree, and not the individuals themselves. So, even if department Y uses only 50 percent of person X's time, person X isn't allowed to decide for themselves how to use the other 50 percent. So, the manager has to go out and look for work. Of course, the reason for that is that it validates the need for the manager.

## A NONDIGITAL TALENT NETWORK

Another approach to liberating talent, one which is human rather than digital, is to encourage workers to organize cross-functional workshops and other events so that people can network and share their skills and knowledge in practical ways in project- or topic-based discussions and exercises. This approach is not yet common in organizations. And it is less empowering than having an internal talent marketplace, where people can participate as they wish. A manager in a retail company explained how they manage finding talent without having a marketplace:

> We are going toward having a project-based organization. Cross-functional workshops are opportunities to network with colleagues from different teams. Then, in case there is a need for a certain skill for the project, it is easier to tap into networks and find the right person.

The lack of examples of talent being valued above roles illustrates that, overall, this is still a weak area for most organizations. As gig mindsetters tend to value talent over roles, they often find themselves at odds with the system.

## Building bridges

Gig-mindset-oriented people are often isolated in the organization. They are frequently surrounded by others who do not understand where they are coming from, why they do what they do.

A senior leader in a European global life sciences company had an idea of how to break through this isolation and help people make connections. Her goal was to get the people on her team to see new perspectives by seeing how other specialists work, their values, and what the other specialists needed. She felt this would build connections in a natural way. She decided to use a familiar structured process to reduce the risk that the new connecting strategy would be rejected. New ideas are more likely to succeed when their approaches are familiar: since the *process* cannot be criticized, that leaves only the idea, the new thing itself.

The leader asked her team members to interview people with specialties very different from their own and to then write a summary of the conversation. She made it a required project, with the results integrated into performance evaluation:

> I brought all of them out of their comfort zone. A technical person got a marketing objective, a good marketing person got an expert in the mathematic calculation of ROI. It was not limited to team members, but across the company, out to completely different areas.
>
> Nearly 30 people all reached out to completely new areas for them. They gained lots of new insights.

After the first time, she no longer had to include the activity in job objectives and performance reviews: her team members were reaching out to others voluntarily. She discovered she had opened minds to a new way of relating to colleagues and had developed new energy in her team. People were breaking out of their traditional mindsets and gradually evolving to a more gig-mindset way of building multidisciplinary teams, with responsibilities defined by skills rather than roles.

In Part 6: "Defining a Perpetual Balance," we look at an approach to navigating the polarities of the traditional and gig mindsets and to finding the right balance in your team, group, or organization. As the title says, the balance is perpetual, constantly changing, making it a challenge to get it right for the given context.

## CASE STUDY: Velcro management in action

BlueShore Financial, based in Vancouver, Canada, offers a range of services in banking, borrowing, wealth management, insurance, and business solutions. The company has 370 employees and has won numerous awards for their work culture.

**The gig-mindset work culture, embodied in Velcro management, bringing out the best in people rather than over-defining roles and hierarchical relations**

A gig-mindset work culture strengthens organizations because it encourages people to go beyond their official job role, to share and live their interests. This builds a strong, flexible, and passionate human infrastructure in the organization. This is the essence of Velcro management and a fundamental part of the gig-mindset work culture.

I discussed management strategies with Marni Johnson, senior vice president, Human Resources and Corporate Affairs, to better understand how they work. I had learned that BlueShore practiced Velcro management and was intrigued to learn more. Joseph L. Bower, in his defining article of 2003, describes Velcro management as a way of ensuring a company is flexible. He writes: "Company management can continuously and effortlessly combine and recombine resources to address new and evolving opportunities that lie across the boundaries of existing business units, while maintaining efficiency in the management of the current business."[9]

### INFRASTRUCTURE OF PEOPLE, NOT ORGANIZATIONAL CHARTS

In today's digital world, a company's infrastructure is determined to a great extent by its management structure. In most organizations, this is described in organizational charts made up of boxes and arrows showing hierarchical flows. Not at BlueShore Financial.

Their approach to management is radically different, and relevant to today's changing, uncertain world of business.

Johnson explained how it works:

> A key element of Velcro management is allowing people to step out of their traditional roles and boundaries, to tap into individuals' strengths and interests to keep them challenged and engaged while at the same time advancing the goals of the business. When we have a business need, and we see we have somebody with a relevant talent and interest, we work with them to incorporate it into their portfolio. And it's always worked for us. With Velcro management, it is your skills and interests that count. You are not confined by your job title.

She gave me an example of how a person working in business support moved to a Learning and Development (L&D) role, then got involved again in her original business unit when the Covid-19 plan was being defined. The combined set of her specific business knowledge and the L&D skills she had acquired made her more immediately valuable than she would have been had she possessed one set but not the other.

## VELCRO MANAGEMENT FACING AN ADAPTIVE CHALLENGE

Adaptive challenges are situations where it is difficult to identify the problem; they cannot be solved by authorities or experts, and the solutions may require experimentation and new discoveries.[10] Often the solution requires changes in beliefs and behaviors. Creating a diverse team fast to address a complex crisis is second nature in a Velcro management context. Johnson described how it happened in the pandemic:

> Our teams really came together to address the Covid-19 pandemic. We were facing an adaptive challenge where there are no known solutions, or many solutions but no clear best choices, and

where the circumstances are constantly changing. We knew that no one person could solve it—it required a team, with very fluid decision-making. We had everyone working very collaboratively and rolling up their sleeves and getting the work done, providing input and improving the overall outcome. We had a shared goal of taking care of our clients, our communities, each other, and our organization now and for the future. The fact that many of our people have diversified experience in different domains was a big plus.

BlueShore's Covid-19-crisis leadership team was organized into five working groups, each one responsible for managing a specific aspect of the crisis. Although each group was led by a subject matter expert, members of the groups reflected their Velcro management approach, with different experiences, specialties, and perspectives. This blend has led to balanced and sound decision-making, as well as to a rich exchange of ideas among and across working groups:

> We have rolled out a number of innovative programs even while managing a crisis. This included more expedited digitization of our business, such as expansion of e-signature capabilities, video-conference client advisory meetings, digital broker account opening, and onboarding of our clients to our digital channels.
>
> We identified unique and creative ways to communicate and engage our staff, clients, and stakeholders at a time where we could not be together [in person]. This involved the virtual Open Mic with staff and executives, a BlueShore-funded employee pay-it-forward program, and our upcoming virtual annual general meeting.

## LEADERS NEED TO SET THE BAR HIGH

Chris Catliff, president and CEO of BlueShore Financial, says that leaders need to "forget the individual's job description and provide them with opportunities to create and contribute to things they excel at and are motivated by."[11]

BlueShore Financial seems to have achieved this. So, my final question to Johnson was about what advice she would give to an organization who wants to implement the Velcro management approach. How to go about it? What should leaders do? What potential obstacles lie in the way, and how can they be overcome?

Her advice, which is both strategic and practical, can be summarized in five key points:

- "First, make sure you are clear on your business strategy and articulate it clearly to all employees. Be relentless in your communication around your strategy. When everyone is aligned and understands where you're going and how they fit into the bigger picture, then everyone can contribute to the maximum.

- "Have an open mindset and look for individuals' skills and interests beyond their job description, and foster that same mindset in your employees so they are proactively looking for new experiences.

- "Nurture an environment of curiosity, and invest in employees' learning. If they are taking on a new area, it's important to provide mentoring, feedback, and an environment that accepts mistakes as learning opportunities.

- "Deliberately curate a culture of collaboration and trust where employees are empowered to provide input, make decisions to move the business forward, and be held accountable for results.

- "Your organizational structure, processes, and practices are key parts of your culture that must not be overlooked. To be effective, they must be consistent with your strategy and desired culture. An example is implementing performance management and rewards systems that facilitate collaboration beyond traditional functional teams."

These recommendations are aligned with a gig-mindset work culture of autonomy, openness, and flexibility. In particular, encouraging people to step outside their official roles and follow their interests, within the framework of the organization's strategy, is liberating and motivating to people with a gig mindset. There is always a new challenge in the organization, and you're free to pursue it!

---

Interview with Marni Johnson, senior vice president, Human Resources and Corporate Affairs. www.blueshorefinancial.com.

# Part 6
## Defining a
## Perpetual Balance

## Navigating polarities, a continual process

IN BRIEF: The gig mindset and the traditional mindset, apparently opposite ways of thinking and behaving, coexist, complement each other, and are interdependent in organizations. They are polarities, two extremes. The appropriate balance will depend on context, which is continually evolving. What follows is an approach to help you find the right balance, and to adjust it as change occurs.

The problem we face is that there is not an appropriate balance between the gig mindset and the traditional mindset in most organizations. The vast majority work nearly completely in the traditional way. There may be individuals or pockets of people here and there who behave in a more gig-mindset mode. They likely face resistance. As we saw in earlier, the reality is that gig mindsetters are rarely recognized, and they may be sidelined because their way of doing things disturbs the status quo.

One solution is to try to have the appropriate mindset at the right time. Gig or traditional? How gig should your organization be? How traditional? Where, when, and how? Different parts of the organization have different processes, goals, and ways of working.

People find themselves struggling between these two approaches when decisions need to be made and actions need to be identified. Discussions turn around questions of the "right" way to reach the goal or solve the problem. Opinions collide and conflict builds. This is because people believe they have a problem to solve and that there is a right way or a wrong way to go about it, as opposed to a wide spectrum of possibilities. Barry Johnson in his *Polarity Management* makes it clear that a narrow right/wrong approach is a counterproductive way to deal with issues.[1]

Polarities are sets of opposites that can't function well independently. Because the two sides of a polarity are interdependent, you cannot choose one as a solution, neglecting the other. The trick is to get the right balance given that particular time. Context is key.

Let's look at an example of polarity mapping, so you see how you might use the approach in your own work context. It is important to remember that the balance between these polarities is not permanent. It needs to be adjusted as contexts evolve. Another important qualifier: this is an approach, not a strict method. It is a way of looking at your situation, and identifying actions in a concerted, structured way.

The four steps outlined below are those I developed based on Johnson's approach. They ideally are done in a workshop with other people. (I guarantee that there will be plenty of discussion!) Once you've worked through the four steps, you will have a specific outcome customized for your organization, a decision-making framework, which serves as a guide for new programs and projects throughout your organization.

*Purpose of Steps 1 and 2:* Become familiar with the gig- versus traditional-mindset concepts.

**Step 1.** Where do you personally fit on the gig–traditional spectrum?

**Step 2.** Where does your organization, department, or team fit on the gig-traditional spectrum? Identify the mindset of your organization, department, or team.

*Purpose of Step 3:* Deepen your understanding of each mindset.

**Step 3.** Identify the upsides and downsides of each mindset. You'll find included here, to stimulate your thinking, material from workshops conducted in cities around the world. But you need to develop your own perceptions, based on yourself and your organization.

*Purpose of Step 4:* Build a customized decision-making framework for your team or organization.

**Step 4.** Set up your real-life polarity matrix to build agreements on how to navigate between the two mindsets based on goals and context. This step is the hardest, and can alone take several hours. Sometimes it is useful to spread it over more than one work session.

## Step 1: Identify where you personally fit on the gig-traditional spectrum

Are you traditional or more gig? Or are you somewhere in between?

Rate yourself (and ask your colleagues to do the same) on a scale of 1 to 5 (with 1 being "fully traditional" and 5 being "fully gig mindset"). This avoids forcing you into one extreme or the other. It's not all or nothing: you can have elements of your mindset that are contradictory—it's human. Circumstances and context influence swings from one mindset to the other, though the data show that people, overall, tend to lean one way more than the other.

Take a look at the eight statements in the table below. Where do you feel the most comfortable? Score yourself on a scale from 1 (traditional mindset) to 5 (gig mindset). Do not hesitate to score yourself at a 2, 3, or 4. When you finish, add up your scores and divide by 8. The resulting number is an indicator of where you fall on the spectrum.

| TRADITIONAL MINDSET | YOUR SCORE, FROM 1 TO 5 | GIG MINDSET |
|---|---|---|
| (1 = TRADITIONAL MINDSET; 5 = GIG MINDSET) | | |
| **1. MOTIVATION** | | |
| I am focused on doing the job using proven and approved methods. | | I prefer out-of-the-box thinking and test-and-learn approaches. |
| **2. ROLES AND SKILLS** | | |
| I feel most comfortable working with people I know, under the leadership of my supervisor, and within the scope of my job role. | | I look for opportunities to work with different types of people in different parts of the organization. I am comfortable with responsibilities defined by skills rather than by roles and hierarchy. |
| **3. OPENNESS** | | |
| I like to progress on a project until an advanced or finished stage before sharing it outside the project team. | | I am comfortable with opening up early, working out loud, and taking feedback from outside the project team as the project advances. |
| **4. AUTONOMY** | | |
| I prefer working under guidance from my supervisor, with decision-making based on hierarchy. | | I often take responsibility for initiating or advancing a project without guidance, and assume responsibility for decisions. |
| **5. QUESTIONING** | | |
| Maintaining stability and consistency in how we do things is very important to me. | | I often challenge the status quo, including business and work practices. |

| TRADITIONAL MINDSET | YOUR SCORE, FROM 1 TO 5 | GIG MINDSET |
|---|---|---|
| **6. AWARENESS** | | |
| I focus primarily on what is happening inside my organization to feed my thinking and my work. | | I am highly aware of what is happening outside my organization that can contribute to my work. I follow what's new in the social, economic, and technology worlds. |
| **7. NETWORKING** | | |
| I tend not to spend time on professional networking, and when I do, it is primarily internal and usually related to the projects I am involved in. | | I do professional networking extensively, building relationships internally and externally. I actively seek interactions with others from whom I learn and to whom I can contribute. |
| **8. ADVANCEMENT** | | |
| My "career path" is important to me. My manager and the HR department are key partners in helping define my future professional evolution. | | My growth path and personal brand are important to me. I am the one primarily responsible for learning and increasing my knowledge and marketable skills. |
| SCORE TOTAL | | |
| SCORE AVERAGE (DIVIDED BY 8) | | |

If your score average is 4 or higher, you are strongly oriented toward a gig mindset; 2 or lower means you tend toward a traditional mindset. If you come out with an average of 3, you are between the two mindsets. It could be that you have a neutral approach in your work life and are comfortable with both extremes, or that the average of 3 results from highs and lows on the different points.

## Step 2: Identify where your group fits on the gig–traditional spectrum

You can do the same analysis of your organization, department, or team using the following table. You'll find that the answers may be quite different across the various parts of your organization.

A large difference between your own score on certain points in Step 1 and the group score in this step explains why you might be feeling discomfort at certain times in your job.

| TRADITIONAL MINDSET | GROUP SCORE, FROM 1 TO 5 | GIG MINDSET |
|---|---|---|
| (1 = TRADITIONAL MINDSET; 5 = GIG MINDSET) | | |
| **1. MOTIVATION** | | |
| Our organization has invested significant time in developing processes covering most aspects of work: performance reviews, client development, HR processes, and other systems and methods. People are expected to follow them as they carry out their work. | | Intrapreneurship and experimentation are part of the organizational culture. People are encouraged to experiment. Management understands that failures will inevitably happen from time to time. Failure is considered a learning opportunity, and people are not sanctioned for breaking the rules or doing things differently. |
| **2. ROLES AND SKILLS** | | |
| Managers and supervisors are considered the people who know best how teams should work and who are best able to define roles and responsibilities among team members. | | Cross-organizational information flows are common, and it is easy to locate people from any part of the organization based on skills (without knowing the person's name). People's roles or position in the hierarchy do not determine their place nor their responsibilities on the team. Roles and responsibilities on the team will likely shift at different points of advancement as different skills are required. |

| TRADITIONAL MINDSET | GROUP SCORE, FROM 1 TO 5 | GIG MINDSET |
|---|---|---|
| | **3. OPENNESS** | |
| The majority of projects in the organization happen in closed spaces. People feel that others will not be interested until their project is finished. They do not want to run the risk of being criticized while the project is ongoing. They want the results to be "perfect" before showing anything to people outside the immediate team, especially people in other parts of the organization. | | Teams willingly make their work visible to the larger organization as they work, and before the work is finished. They work out loud by using internal social and communication channels or simply having project walls visible to people passing by. They solicit feedback from people outside the team who may have information, ideas, or contacts that will enrich the outcome or even help anticipate potential issues. |
| | **4. AUTONOMY** | |
| Each person defers to the person who is one step higher in the hierarchy. Decisions are made at a given level, then flow down the chain, level by level. This brings consistency and control across the organization. | | People are free to identify issues and find ways to deal with them. This may be done through ad hoc projects and teams. People assume responsibility for the outcome: they are convinced there is a real need and that they, with the help of a team or group around them, can come up with a solution to a challenge or invent new ways of working. |
| | **5. QUESTIONING** | |
| Our organization focuses on stability and consistency in how we work. We have invested significant time in defining processes and ways of working. People have been trained, and we have been successful. There is no reason to change something that works well. | | Challenging the status quo is anchored in actions: finding new ways of doing business and new work practices that bring value to the organization. A new practice may let people work faster, more efficiently, improve something such as quality or client satisfaction, or help achieve something that was previously impossible. |

| TRADITIONAL MINDSET | GROUP SCORE, FROM 1 TO 5 | GIG MINDSET |
|---|---|---|
| **6. AWARENESS** | | |
| We have everything we need inside our organization. Our workforce includes a diversity of people with different skills and knowledge. With our internal knowledge combined, we have a broad awareness of the world. | | Things happening in the external world that are directly or indirectly related to what we do are part of the big picture of which we are all part. People do not exist in isolation, nor does our organization. We have systematic ways of observing and sharing what people see around them at conferences and other industry events. |
| **7. NETWORKING** | | |
| Networking internally with close and distant colleagues is sufficient for us to build our knowledge together. It is important to communicate and share information internally and, when appropriate, to connect our internal networks together. | | Internal and external networks are equally valued as sources of information. The boundaries between the two are fluid, and contacts outside can be as useful as contacts inside. We have systematic ways of sharing internally what we learn from external sources. |
| **8. ADVANCEMENT** | | |
| People in our organization are hired do a job and to acquire more skills so they can progress in their careers. People want to move up the ladder, whether in responsibility, status, or salary, or all three. They count on HR and their managers to help them achieve this. | | People take ownership of their learning and personal growth. Our organization thinks in terms of an internal marketplace where people's expertise, experience, and capabilities give them opportunities to participate in and contribute to different projects inside the organization as they cultivate and grow their own brands. |
| SCORE TOTAL | | |
| SCORE AVERAGE (DIVIDED BY 8) | | |

If the score average is 4 or higher, the group is strongly oriented toward a gig mindset. A score average of 2 or lower means it leans more toward a traditional mindset. As with the individual scores discussed above, an average of 3 needs to be examined to see if it results from highs and lows on the different points or represents an overall neutral way of working. The former is worth looking at in detail to understand if some traits should be focused on and targeted for change initiatives. The latter, with all traits rated in the middle, deserves reflection, as it raises the question of whether the organizational culture is one of stagnation, "sitting on the fence" and unable to evolve, or if it is the result of a slow general evolution one way or the other.

## Step 3: Identify the upsides and downsides of each mindset

This section provides you with feedback from people in different contexts to stimulate your own thinking once you identify the upsides and downsides of the two mindsets in your own context, as you will do in Step 4.

Workshops were organized in different cities around the world to dig into perceptions of the upsides and downsides of both mindsets from a range of industries and countries. The chart below is a high-level summary of the 11 workshops.

You can see a description of the detailed output in Appendix A2: "Upsides and Downsides."

Overall, the upsides of the traditional mindset are that it represents a sense of stability, comfort, belonging, and personal security. The gig-mindset upsides, on the other hand, reflect movement, empowerment, speed, and openness to the world.

When it comes to downsides, the stable, consistent traditional mindset is behind the hesitation to embrace change, as well as a lack of engagement for work environments where there is strict management without the values of true leadership. The gig mindset has downsides as well. The movement encompassed by the upsides can end up being too fast, thereby causing quality problems. It can also

|  | TRADITIONAL MINDSET | GIG MINDSET |
|---|---|---|
| **UPSIDES** | People understand the organization and where they belong. | Effective and happy employees, because they are more empowered. |
|  | People feel comfortable and do not take risks. | Inspires and attracts talent: lower HR costs because people manage their development. |
|  | Creates a work culture that can be more easily influenced. | Strong capacity for innovation; evolution of products and services means faster growth. |
|  | Brings stability, security, and protection, which motivate and build loyalty. | Openness and curiosity about successful initiatives outside the organization. |
| **DOWNSIDES** | Management by orders, no or little leadership: "Big Brother is watching you." | Testing and learning can create too many cycles, slowing the project and worrying leaders. |
|  | Difficulty in adapting to the external, changing environment. | Gig mindsetters can be perceived poorly by hierarchy and colleagues. |
|  | Higher risk of final project/service not being usable. | Problem of stability of quality in mass services. |
|  | Teams are unprepared in case of big change. | Higher turnover: loss of knowledge, difficult long-term planning. |

create concern and lack of confidence from managers and peers, and even higher turnover and loss of talent as gig mindsetters move elsewhere.

The workshop facilitators shared observations from their sessions that show us the depth and breadth of the conversations. They reported that industries "fearing disruption" have seen a surge in the number of gig mindsetters brought in to help foster new and innovative ideas, ways of working, products, and so on. In finance, for example, they interestingly don't fear each other, but are uneasy about the "new kids on the block," such as fintech startups and small incumbents providing better banking experiences.

One response to this is to simply acquire the skills and knowledge they haven't been able to grow internally themselves. Those acquisitions often come with a number of new hires in the gig-mindset category. A different type of leadership is then needed, one that is more of a coaching role than a traditional command-and-control management role. Still, many of the most talented gig-mindset hires have a tendency to disappear if new owners integrate their smaller unit too deeply into the larger corporation. The result of these changes triggers potential conflict of work cultures, as these quotes describe:

> The gig mindset is nothing new—organizations bringing products or services to market have always needed people with this mindset. But the pace at which senior leaders wish to bring those in, and the churn of people with these characteristics, has increased enormously, leading to frictions, a sense of uncertainty, and so on, within the existing frameworks.

> Onboarding in the "mixed reality" with gig + traditional intake is hard—the gig mindset doesn't fit with the onboarding often designed for the established roles and structures. Should they be taken through a different process, integrated in a different way, or introduced to the same things? Should it take the same amount of time?

> What happens when gig mindsetters underperform and there are no checks? How do you manage underperformers in gig mindset? It's harder without the traditional roles and responsibilities.

> There are more meetings with gig mindsetters. So much time often wasted. People with a traditional mindset know what has to be done, so they just do it.

## WORK CULTURES IN TRANSITION

When an organization hires a large number of new workers or makes an acquisition in order to get workers who are already gig-mindset oriented, the issues triggered in these periods of fast transition have no absolute solutions. These issues came up frequently in the workshops:

- Uncertainty is felt by current workers when organizations bring in new gig mindsetters.

- High turnover is experienced with gig mindsetters, a result of high demand in the marketplace.

- The need for a coaching style of management rather than traditional command-and-control style.

- Concern about evaluating the performance of gig mindsetters, particularly when they underperform, since traditional roles and responsibilities may no longer apply.

- Meaningful success criteria for teams made up either entirely of gig-mindset hires or a combination of existing employees and gig-mindset hires.

- Lack of efficiency with gig mindsetters, who tend toward discussion and meetings rather than just getting on and doing what has to be done without asking questions.

- Recognition that there may be new ways to onboard gig mindsetters, and that the traditional processes may no longer be appropriate.

These questions require thought, discussion, and, ideally, sharing with other people in your organization. The result will give your input for Step 4.

## Step 4: Set up your real-life polarity matrix

In this step, you gain a greater ability to define actions that work toward your goals, helping you navigate in the direction you want to go and providing guidelines for decision-making.

What follows is a series of substeps to go through as a group. You can do them in any order and will certainly find yourselves working back and forth from point to point, revising and refining as you advance.

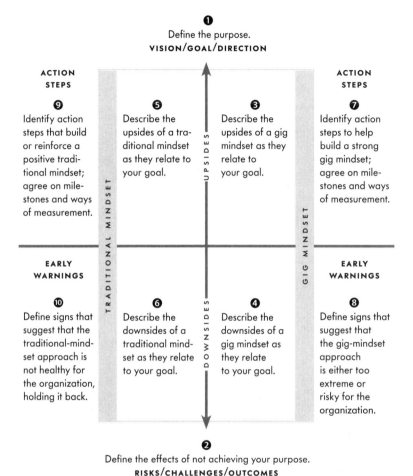

**❶**
Define the purpose.
VISION/GOAL/DIRECTION

**ACTION STEPS** (left) — **ACTION STEPS** (right)

**❾**
Identify action steps that build or reinforce a positive traditional mindset; agree on milestones and ways of measurement.

**❺**
Describe the upsides of a traditional mindset as they relate to your goal.

**❸**
Describe the upsides of a gig mindset as they relate to your goal.

**❼**
Identify action steps to help build a strong gig mindset; agree on milestones and ways of measurement.

TRADITIONAL MINDSET — UPSIDES — GIG MINDSET

**EARLY WARNINGS** (left) — **EARLY WARNINGS** (right)

**❿**
Define signs that suggest that the traditional-mindset approach is not healthy for the organization, holding it back.

**❻**
Describe the downsides of a traditional mindset as they relate to your goal.

**❹**
Describe the downsides of a gig mindset as they relate to your goal.

**❽**
Define signs that suggest that the gig-mindset approach is either too extreme or risky for the organization.

DOWNSIDES

**❷**
Define the effects of not achieving your purpose.
RISKS/CHALLENGES/OUTCOMES

## ADJUST BASED ON EARLY WARNINGS

When early warning signs occur, whether for the gig mindset or the traditional mindset, you need to reinforce the actions identified previously, for the benefit of the opposite side. In the example illustrated in the chart below, an early warning sign for the gig mindset is clients asking for more and more new features while the project is ongoing, making the project undeliverable. One way to approach this is to look at the action steps for the traditional mindset, such as using project managers with more experience in managing client expectations or defining deliverables more precisely, or reviewing the initial scope statement.

**❶**
**Purpose: Become and remain an innovative, market-leading organization**

**❾ Identify action steps, milestones, evaluation**

Use experienced project managers.

Define deliverables at the start.

Determine reporting systems and timing.

Etc.

**❺ Describe the upsides**

Projects have predefined deliverables.

People work with proven procedures and methods.

Roles and responsibilities are clear.

People get up to speed fast.

Time is invested in improving existing systems.

**❸ Describe the upsides**

Creative, out-of-the-box thinking for experimental projects.

Able to change in direction as unexpected events happen.

More fulfilling work.

Strong sense of team and individual contributions.

High awareness of external environment.

**❼ Identify action steps, milestones, evaluation**

Work closely with customers.

Give people more autonomy.

Celebrate successes.

Accept failures and share the learning.

Etc.

*UPSIDES* — *TRADITIONAL MINDSET* — *GIG MINDSET*

**❿ Identify early warning signs**

Talented, experienced people are leaving the organization.

Clients are complaining about late deliveries.

Etc.

**❻ Describe the downsides**

No freedom to innovate, propose, and test new ideas.

Work takes longer; progress may be slow.

Lots of permission-seeking.

Management by orders, no or little leadership except hierarchical.

**❹ Describe the downsides**

Testing and learning can create too many cycles, slowing the project.

Business leaders may be uncomfortable with uncertain results.

Problem of stability of quality with too many customized versions of the product.

**❽ Identify early warning signs**

Project manager unable to predict delivery date.

Managers are considering outsourcing the work.

Clients are asking for more and more new features while project is in progress.

*DOWNSIDES*

**❷**
**Risk of not achieving our purpose: Being vulnerable to new competitors**

## RESULTS: MANAGE DISAGREEMENTS, ACHIEVE FLEXIBILITY

The steps outlined on the chart above are intended to give you a sense of how to navigate the polarities of the gig mindset versus the traditional mindset flexibly, without falling into extreme disagreements, or worse still, meaningless consensus. This approach frees people to disagree in a tangible, reasoned way, and enables them to envisage alternative actions from the start. It makes decision-making for projects and activities easier for all involved because there is a framework to fall back on, a framework that is adjustable based on needs.

## CASE STUDY: Entrepreneurship in a bimodal work culture

A global agricultural commodity trading company (referred to as ACTC to respect its request for anonymity) works in a bimodal culture.

### A strong gig-mindset culture thriving in a traditional-mindset context

The gig mindset and the traditional mindset are, at first glance, opposites. In fact, they are polarities: interdependent and complementary. Whereas most organizations have insufficient gig-mindset behaviors, ACTC has found the right balance. The teams that work in gig-mindset mode rely on those that represent a traditional way of working, and vice versa. Together, they flourish.

For ACTC, it is a question of having a gig mindset alongside a traditional mindset, not gig versus traditional. Too often we think of the negative aspects of the traditional mindset and the positive aspects of the gig mindset. This is an oversimplification, and this case illustrates how the two mindsets intertwine.

## A WORKPLACE OF IMPERMANENCE WITH OPPORTUNITIES COMING AND GOING

The bimodal work culture is a deliberate part of ACTC's strategy.

The front office is made up of two types of workers: traders who do the deals, and support staff who execute the trading orders and make the deals happen. People in these latter jobs are by nature adaptive. A deal can collapse in three minutes or be radically transformed. If that happens, the trader moves on to the next deal.

For example, the trader makes a deal selling coffee beans, then the support people figure out the logistics for getting the coffee onto a boat and off to its destination. A competitor or another company may buy it before it arrives at the destination. This may happen five or six times before the boat reaches its final destination. These people are in a workplace of—in one word—*impermanence*. There is constant movement. They have a gig-mindset way of working by the very nature of their job. Autonomy, awareness of the external world, initiatives, improvisation, and speed are strong dimensions of their work culture.

Other people in the company, known as the back office, working in support functions such as HR or finance, have more traditional methods, processes, and tools. The back-office work culture is based on stability, proven methods, and well-established procedures. They use agreed-upon tools and structured solutions, which is essential because they are integrated into company-wide practices. In contrast, the tools used by the traders are based on individual choices and include WhatsApp, Jabber, and custom-made Excel spreadsheets.

## TRADITIONAL IN THE BACK, GIG IN THE FRONT, WORKING TOGETHER

Having these two different digital work environments is a deliberate choice on the part of ACTC. Front office must be able to react fast to customers and market changes, and the back office must be stable and consistent, functioning as expected, with no surprises.

The value ACTC delivers is in trading and trading management. Even factories and plants are considered assets and part of the support functions, not part of the heart of the business. A factory or plant is seen as a pure asset because it can be decided overnight that it is no longer essential and is therefore sold. The factory is there to transform raw material when needed, so little investment is made in it. It is seen as a commodity.

## DISRUPTION, IMPROVISATION, AND SPEED

The commodity market is impacted by what happens in the external world—trade wars, sanctions, diseases, geopolitical tensions. A trade war between the US and China creates disruption for companies like ACTC. An anti-French movement in the US may result in Americans saying they don't want foie gras or wine from France. An illness in Africa may cause the flow of commodities to change quickly. This is because silos that have been bought and corresponding agreements with partners for stocking or transforming products may no longer viable.

In the case of ACTC, the business of trading US soybeans with clients in China was abruptly interrupted for political reasons. It was essential to find a new solution fast, since soybeans can't be stored for months on end. The solution, found by a young trader, was to transform the soybeans into soybean meal, a key ingredient of fodder. The trader found a new partner to make the transformation, then was able to sell it on as a food for cattle and other animals.

Traders must be able to switch strategies fast. They might sell the product but in a different country, or transform it, to be used for a different purpose, as in the previous example. Traders need to be flexible when faced with a complex situation with new, unexpected needs. They do what they have to do to make it work. Value is finding the right buyer at the right time in a constantly changing world of opportunities.

The entrepreneurial culture is important to ACTC. A trader who makes a commercial breakthrough may well be recognized by being promoted to country manager or platform manager. ("When I was I trader…" conversations can be heard around the coffee machines.) Such traders are also celebrated in corporate announcements, where their achievements are described. Whereas, in many companies, announcements are that a newly promoted director was key in building a quality program or developing a marketing strategy, at ACTC, it's all about business: the trader opened a new business, transformed an old market into a new business, opened a new country, negotiated a new partnership, and so on. Adaptability, flexibility, and speed are at the heart of the business. They are also at the heart of how a gig mindsetter works.

# Part 7
## Owning Your
## Personal Strategy

---

IN BRIEF: The gig mindset is an identity, a way of understanding yourself. In a world of job insecurity, building a strong individual identity can be a smart risk-management strategy at the individual level. It will determine how you manage your work life inside an organization, or how you operate if you choose to go independent. It will also help you manage things if you had not planned to leave your organization but suddenly find yourself in the job market after unexpected events. Strengthening your personal development as you work in your organization may help you be more marketable externally as well as internally, should you be impacted by downsizing, restructuring, or a merger.

A technology expert working in the financial industry who found himself suddenly on the job market talked about labels versus skills:

I think a lot of people would struggle if they were to lose their job in their present situation because they are identified by the label that is their job, rather than by their skill set.

Another interviewee, although she has been in the same company for many years, emphasized the importance of having a gig mindset for future security:

Given where the world is going, I believe everybody needs to work toward developing a gig mindset, because the future of work is so up in the air. Things are changing so fast that working with a traditional mindset, where you're doing things the way you always have, will not let you position yourself very well for future career success. It might work in your current job, but I don't think it is sustainable long term.

We know that people are no longer guaranteed permanent employment in their organization. Previous social contracts are unraveling. This means people need to think about what they want. Jon Husband, who defined the wirearchy concept, phrases it as a fundamental choice analogous to dating or committing long term:

This is not unlike the dance between dating and long-term commitment to a relationship. So, a lot of people, consciously or not, have taken in that message and are saying, "Well, why should I owe loyalty to an employer? I need to work to pay the mortgage, to feed the kids, and so on. But they just basically told me they're not going to commit to me, so why should I commit to them in any way other than somewhat perfunctory?"

Some find this approach perfectly logical. If it's a question of loyalty, loyalty to whom?

A research participant from Denmark who considers herself to be strongly oriented to the gig mindset spoke of the importance of making a difference:

I find myself being more loyal to myself and where I believe I can make a difference, rather than being loyal to a company or a manager.

There is a lot of talk today about how younger generations are not looking for longtime commitments. Some believe it is a question of age and that young people in all times have been eager to change often, move around, try different jobs and employers. They believe that younger people entering the workforce do not expect nor want a job for life. Others say it stems from the reality younger people see around them today: constant change, uncertainties, economic downturns in certain industries and regions. When I finished university, I had no doubt that I would find an interesting, permanent job. Now, several decades later, this is clearly no longer the case for young people.

An experienced worker in his early forties talked about how the younger people in his organization have a nomadic mindset:

I have a feeling that people who are younger around me in the workplace have a more open mindset—looking outside, not purely focusing on the internal organization. People in my generation feel like the organization is a family—and I'm part of the family. The young people are more pragmatic—they're here for a while, don't want to commit their whole life to the organization. They're learning, they move somewhere, they might be working with the organization as an independent or on temporary loan from another organization.

People with expertise that is in high demand can negotiate and move around easily. This is especially the case in geographical areas where there are clusters of specialized organizations. However, even this is evolving. For example, in our era of dependency on algorithms, mathematicians are now more in demand than engineers in Silicon Valley.

Whichever choice you make—dating or long-term commitment—you need, as a gig mindsetter, to give thought to your personal strategy and path. As we saw in the opening of the book, gig mind-setters are often uncomfortable in traditional organizations. They can often make those with a more traditional mindset feel uneasy, and they themselves feel their value is neither recognized nor appreciated. If that's the case for you, you have three potential directions to take, each with a different outcome:

- The first is the **advocate** path. Find ways to demonstrate that your ways of working bring worthwhile outcomes. Live the gig-mindset way of working inside your organization and inspire people around you. Help them see new ways of working for themselves as well.

- The second is the **compromise** path. Find acceptable solutions for how you work in order to fit into the work culture while not sacrificing too much integrity and sense of self. This takes will power, resignation, a high degree of common sense, or all three.

- The third is the **exit** path. Leave the organization and look for other opportunities, either a salaried position in another organization or as an independent freelancer.

## The advocate path: The hardest and riskiest

More than 10 years of research on the internal digital work environment has shown me that one of the highest, if not the highest, change driver in organizations is "behavior of my colleagues"—with "behavior of senior management" nearly as high. The gig-mindset behavior can be contagious. Can you, with a gig-mindset attitude, help others see things, work, and interact differently? That is a hard one. Your challenge is to get senior managers to understand that the more they decentralize and the more they trust the people at the edges of the organization, the easier it is to develop a gig-mindset work culture. This makes it more likely that the organization will be resilient in the face of crises and will evolve successfully.

If you're able to influence even one person in a powerful position in your organization, you may be in luck. That person can become your stepping-stone to other senior people. Of course, there is always the risk that, if at some point that person is no longer there, their successor may have a different, even potentially negative, approach to your work. It is therefore crucial to take two precautions:

- Develop your contact with more than one senior person. If one changes, you can hopefully count on the others to support you. However, if your primary connection is with the CEO, who then leaves, it may be difficult to ensure support from senior people working directly under the new CEO.

- Establish as many structural means as possible to cultivate and sustain gig-mindset-oriented initiatives. This includes physical traditions such as lunches or evening events on a regular basis with external guests. Virtual structures such as online communities and networks are more likely to outlive changes in top management because they are "invisible" and attract less attention than do face-to-face events.

## LITTLE STEPS LEAD TO BIG MOMENTUM

Another way to build a strong individual identity inside an organization is to communicate in the internal social network and get people to connect around your ideas. As a senior manager in a life sciences company said:

> I suspect that it's a language of networks rather than individuals. If you find the right people to connect with, people who can spread that sort of thinking, then it becomes a part of how we do business. And it's not necessarily people high up in the hierarchy that need to do that. It could be anywhere, really, I think . . . But at some point, someone has to go, "I get this and I'm going to do it."

Change initiatives are likely already happening in your organization. Find ways to bring them out into the open. The internal social network is a starting point. An employee at a European industrial company told me how he and a colleague had built momentum for change by creating a sense of community among people across the organization:

> We started building a community by having a spontaneous online meeting that anyone could join to propose ideas of what kind of action we could do with this community. Then we had a vote and made those actions into a priority list of things to do that year. This was in 2017. Some of those things became real, like creating a network of sparring partners to help each other out.
>
> We believe that change comes from the fringe. Let's demonstrate what we are already doing, and let's make it inclusive so others can see. We organized a two-hour meeting in a very large outside space. Between one hundred and two hundred people turned up, with food and drinks, a few signs, and a few stands. It was divided into Take Action, Learn and Share, and things like that.
>
> None of these people had an official job that had anything to do with change and new ways of working. One of the top senior leaders came over and actually asked, "Why is all of this happening from you people and not from HR?"
>
> Basically, we believe we've started a grassroots movement for people taking responsibility for changing the company. After this event, we decided that rather than just waiting around and complaining about things and trying to argue using logic, we should just get out and do it.

### BEWARE THE GIG-MINDSET EGO TRAP

When a gig mindsetter has achieved something outstanding and has been recognized for it, and the effort required to achieve it has been huge, it is only human to want to share the story externally as well. It is important that the story of individual achievement is balanced with recognition of the teams involved or the organization itself.

For example, let's say you think your achievement would be a good case study to share at a conference, or use as a subject for an article in a business publication. Depending on how the story is spun, it can create a good impression or a negative image of your organization. The first may not be accurate, especially if they recognized the value only after the initiative was a success. The second may be nearer the truth but may well cause legal problems for you unless precautions were taken every step of the way during the project.

That is a risk if the achievement involved shortcuts or bypassing enterprise processes. If the story is publicized externally, the organization may feel a need—or even be advised by legal counsel—to silence the story. I know of two such cases. One was solved amicably, with a mutually agreed time-off period, the other ended with threats, lawyers, and departure indemnities for a forced resignation. In the second case, the gig mindsetter had squashed any future opportunities with the organization. They also cannot refer to their significant accomplishment in a professional reference, only in anecdotal personal conversations. In the first case, the person was to join a leading-edge research team because of their unique expertise, which was recognized and missed once they left the organization.

In both cases, the organization benefited from the gig mindsetter's initiative, but the outcomes were radically different. This is in part a result of personalities, the industries involved, and the degree of external visibility of each case. Company regulations may come into play too, depending on what is done publicly and what happens inside corporate walls. In one global industrial company, two employees piloted an internal talent marketplace on Facebook and LinkedIn, just to see how it would work. They had not notified their managers. They could have run it internally as a test, but it was easier and faster for them to use the external social media platforms. Not surprisingly, they were both soon looking for new jobs! They had unintentionally exposed employees in the organization to talent poachers from other companies. Their speed worked against them.

In another example, the gig mindsetter posted a public Facebook page to attract worldwide attention to a particular cause. Knowing that if she asked permission, it would be denied, she went ahead and created the Facebook page in the name of the company. Within just a few days, thousands of people had "liked" the page. The company was admired and thanked for the initiative. It was perceived as a leader worldwide thanks to the Facebook page. Other companies in the industry soon got on board, and several programs and practical actions took place over the following months. Despite not following procedures, the gig mindsetter who posted the page was praised and admired.

So, internal or external visibility? Permission or just do it? Each case is different and has its risks and merits.

## The compromise path: A negotiation with yourself

Are you both of a traditional and a gig mindset, depending on place, time, context, and even mood? An architect I interviewed had recently joined a government agency after working a decade at a private firm. She found that the context she was in, including the role and skills of her coworkers, meant that she could no longer function sufficiently as a creative, freelance-style architect. In addition to design, she now had to complete paperwork for standards and other administrative requirements. She felt frustrated and bored and was unsure how long she would stay at the agency. The position involved a mismatch of skills: those required for stability and consistency and those fueled by the desire to create designs. The architect had options: accept doing more administrative work; negotiate an arrangement with colleagues who are not bothered or even enjoy the administrative work; or leave the position. Of course, the other options are to stay there with no changes, frustrated and bored, or find peace of mind that both dimensions are necessary and worthwhile for her to do.

Like the architect, you may work in an area where you need to demonstrate both qualities. When we look at polarities, that raises another dimension. One polarity can live inside the other. For example, certain actions within larger activities require stability and consistency, while others require out-of-the-box thinking. Stability is important for monitoring, reporting, evaluating, and measuring. Thinking creatively and challenging the status quo is important for

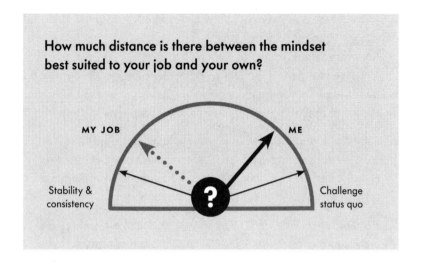

How much distance is there between the mindset best suited to your job and your own?

MY JOB

ME

Stability & consistency

Challenge status quo

analyzing inputs, conducting needs analyses, and brainstorming ideas. You may well find that you need both qualities in your work. Or you may find that your job and your qualities are a mismatch.

### BALANCE YOUR OWN POLARITIES

One way to gain clarity on your own situation is to use the traditional-versus gig-mindset table on page 134: Step 1, Identify where you personally fit on the gig–traditional spectrum. Reflect on the eight statements in the table scoring them for yourself (see page 133 for the table and instructions). Then go through the same statements, scoring them for a hypothetical "ideal person" who could do your job and fit well into your organizational work culture. How much difference is there between the two scores? If there is a big difference, look at which behaviors vary the most and determine if they are important for you. If so, think of specific examples for each behavior; you will be able to see, in more concrete terms, if there is a change you can make to the context, to the job itself, or to your way of working. Or is it something you just have to live with if you stay in that job? Breaking the differences down into smaller parts and real mini-examples will make your analysis easier than if you look at the big picture and conclude "I can't stay here."

Between the extremes of a focus on stability and the frequent challenging of the status quo, where do you fit most of the time? And is your job and work culture oriented in that way most of the time?

Here's an exchange I observed in a Slack group discussion:

Person 1. What I wonder is why do people with a gig mindset stay with the organization? I did not. After a handful of internal successes, I decided that I could do this as an independent for many organizations—why stick with one?

Person 2. The answer to "Why stick with one?" is stability and consistency of work—70 percent of one's work may be working in a gig-mindset or adaptive-team model, but the other 30 percent is what I call "stacked" work, meaning you are supporting management and organizational needs.

Interestingly, both of these people left their organizations. The first became a globally known expert in his field, often called in to organizations for short, strategic missions. The second worked on longer contracts for very large organizations, helping them through changes such as mergers or opening new markets. The difference in their subsequent situations—short and strategic missions versus longer-term constructing missions—corresponds perfectly to their answers to the question "Why stay in the organization?"

## OVERCOME THE BARRIERS IN YOUR MIND

People are so used to working within constraints that ingrained habits and reflexes are hard to change, as described by an engineer who has spent a lot of time observing people in his organization:

Actually, what we realized is that in an organization like ours, there is a significant amount of freedom. It's just that people don't believe there is.

People fear the insecurity, or the instability, of what you call the gig mindset. They've got used to having a box around what they do and leaving the responsibility with the manager.

A senior director for a company providing technology solutions for the education market talked about the personal challenge people experience when change happens. He refers to it as "an inner fear, an inner monologue." The company changed their sales strategy from selling products and features to outcome selling—selling to vertical markets where a key part of the sales process is negotiating outcomes with executives. This differs significantly from selling features to IT directors. According to the director,

> Not all salespeople feel comfortable. They think "I might not be as successful selling as I used to be." That inner fear, that inner monologue, can sometimes be very loud. That is a personal challenge.

A chief development and communications officer at a not-for-profit organization spoke about how going digital was much more than a cultural change. For his organization, it became personal:

> Not only did we have to change the culture but we had to deal with fear. It was really important for us to get to the root of that, to understand everybody's different perspective, especially the fear of "I won't be able to learn this."

## FIND AN OUTLET FOR YOUR GIG MINDSET

Several people talked to me about how having an activity or small business on the side satisfies their gig-mindset spirit. It helps them stay in their traditional roles in traditional companies, which they need to do for financial or personal reasons. One person believed it was a question of age and economy:

> Age and geographical economies are factors to my work style. In my early career, I was very organizationally focused. In later years, I successfully experimented and enjoyed a gig-thinking approach, until [there was] a downturn in available jobs. I am now back at a large corporation and blend my approaches where appropriate because I can read situations now due to experience. And I operate a small side business that fulfills my gig thinking.

In places like the US, where not all employers offer healthcare, it becomes a reason for staying in a job:

> The place where I work 9-5 is very different in culture, values, and vision from the work I do outside. I occasionally work as an adviser, sometimes volunteer, sometimes paid, for a society of participatory medicine, and with a startup for adolescent and family mental health. The key reason I remain at my day-job employer is healthcare, because I have significant preexisting conditions with family members, and kids in college, who utilize my healthcare... I feel I can't change my primary career until one of the organizations I'm helping can become funded and offer healthcare.

## The exit path: Tough yet potentially the most fulfilling

Finding a salaried job in another organization is hard to do, especially if you don't have it lined up before you leave your current one. The job market has evolved, and for many people, the only real opportunity is setting up as an independent freelancer and starting your own business.

Of five people I spoke with over recent months who opted for the exit path, two set up as freelancers, two joined small organizations, and one took a year-long time-off period, returning before it ended to work on a strategic project, at the request of his previous manager. This is a rare example of where the distance the time off provided worked well for both parties. The employee had time to reflect and attempt to build a new career as an entrepreneur, which he was unable to do, unsurprisingly, in such a short timeframe. The organization, represented by the manager, realized, "Hey, we need this guy!" The two freelancers had short-term agreements with their previous employer for a few months of work, so they had some breathing space. The two who joined small organizations seem to be doing well so far.

New freelancers need to ask themselves a fundamental question: Can I transfer my experience as an insider, as I was in my previous job, to different contexts and companies where I will be an outsider, as an external consultant, for instance? Consider how will you position yourself in front of potential clients. If you left your organization feeling fed up or discouraged, you'll need to be careful to project a positive, energetic impression to potential employers. If you left with relief, new ideas, and energy, along with references, that will obviously be easier.

## TRANSFORMATIONAL LEADERSHIP, FROM THE OUTSIDE IN

You can be an outsider when you're inside an organization. You can be an insider when you're outside an organization. The distinction is not always clear-cut. You may be such a valued adviser that you have more inside knowledge and impact on the organization than do many of the true insiders. I have experienced the insider role two or three times in an 18-year career as an adviser to large organizations. This role does not usually last more than two or three years because it makes management nervous; they're unwilling to have so much dependence on an outsider. Also, if you are doing your work well, you'll be sharing your skills with your insider colleagues, who gradually will be able to play the role you are playing. This is the essence of transformational leadership, where a leader (in this case, you) works closely with others (your client team), defining a vision and inspiring those around them to be part of the movement to reach the goals.[1] In the process, those working with you, "the leader," develop their own identity and are able to confidently take ownership of the work. This is perhaps the most powerful and genuine way a gig mindsetter, working outside the organization but acting as an insider, can bring lasting benefits to people inside the organization and to the organization itself.

# Finding your place in the shamrock

The term "shamrock organization" comes from the Irish author and management philosopher Charles Handy.[2] The shamrock, a national emblem of Ireland, is a clover-like plant with three leaves that represent three groups of workers in Handy's metaphor:

1. The first leaf is the core of essential managers and full-time workers, which Handy refers to as the professional core. They represent the organization in that they own the knowledge that distinguishes the organization from others. They think in terms of careers and are paid based on organizational performance.

2. The second leaf is what Handy calls the contractual fringe. It is made up of self-employed people, including freelancers, and other organizations (usually smaller than the contracting client), offering specific talent, expertise, or services. They are paid by fees rather than by time, based on deliverables, on a project-by-project basis.

3. The third leaf is a flexible, contingent workforce—part time or temporary—who perform routine jobs as needed according to seasonal demand. They are usually paid by the hour, day, or week. They think in terms of jobs, not careers, and often expect no more than reasonable pay and work conditions.

Handy adds a fourth group, worth mentioning in passing though not directly related to our topic: the customer. There are many examples of customers doing work that was previously done by employees: bagging their groceries, filling their cars with gas, using ATMs to bank, and buying furniture, then renting a vehicle through the company to drive home and assemble what they bought. Much of this is done in the name of customer convenience and lower prices.

## WHERE DOES THE GIG MINDSET FIT IN THE SHAMROCK ORGANIZATION?

Being a gig mindsetter and part of the first leaf—the professional core—is tricky. People are expected to show unflinching loyalty to the organization. This can be difficult for a gig mindsetter, for whom challenging the status quo is part of how they attempt to bring about change. People in this group tend to focus on their career path, a series of different job assignments which they go through, moving either up the corporate ladder or sideways. People moving sideways are developing as experts and will be sought after for their knowledge and experience. People moving upward become high-level managers and heads of departments. Whichever way they move, gig mindsetters in the professional core group will have high visibility in their work and need to find a way to advance their philosophy of work in contexts that are sometimes overly traditional.

Whether moving upward or sideways, they have less security than in the past. Companies are downsizing, restructuring, merging, acquiring, or being acquired. The internal job landscape is constantly shifting, including at the top of the hierarchy and in expertise positions, as organizations exit or enter markets reactively or proactively in their competitive landscape.

As part of this group, gig mindsetters will almost always face obstacles, struggle to work within organizational constraints, or do their utmost to bring about change in the organization. Some succeed, others do not.

However, if you're on the advocate path, being part of the first leaf can be a powerful starting point for influencing colleagues and management to change the way they work.

In the end, though, you may find yourself on the compromise path, as discussed earlier. As a gig mindsetter, you either manage to mobilize people around new ways of working or you end up compromising your gig values and finding a personal and professional balance in other ways.

If you, as a gig mindsetter, are in the second leaf, part of the contractual fringe, it means you have either never worked in an organization or have left one and are working on contract basis, either on your own or with another company. You are in charge of your advancement and need a continual strategy of learning and self-development.

This can be more secure than the first leaf, with one major condition: that you have skills that are in demand. Although you are not salaried by the company you are doing work for, and therefore may not have the safety net of permanent work nor access to healthcare and unemployment benefits, you may be able to find as much work as you want if you have rare skills or skills for which there is a large need. Needs fluctuate. In the past, technology software engineers were in high demand. Today, it's mathematicians. This is not surprising when we think about the extent to which statistical analysis is used in decisions made by companies.[3]

Your gig mindset will mean you are probably an active networker and have invested in developing new skills. You have lots of contacts and a strong reputation. You may be part of an agency that sells your services as a contractor, or you may be independent.

Over my years of working with large global organizations, I regularly received requests to connect on LinkedIn. Sometimes the person sending the invitation had left the organization or was planning to go. Unfortunately, that's late in the game to start networking—but better late than never.

Several of the gig mindsetters I interviewed prefer being part of the second leaf. They tend to have in-demand skills and can move from project to project, from client to client, internally or externally, learning and acquiring additional skills as they go. This represents a continual strategy of self-development and learning.

A gig mindsetter based in Silicon Valley said:

> I've seen the shift toward creating a knowledge workforce that is more contingent. Those individuals not only master their networks to survive, they also are often moving across organizations from project to project and therefore gaining more varied experience, knowledge, and organizational insight than individuals in traditional roles. In that kind of climate, the digital and social models of work practice become important for sustaining access to knowledge. You see the tacit knowledge exchanges in the context of work. You learn by doing in the natural flow of work.

The third leaf, the contingent workforce, with its routines and common skills, is not an ideal group for a gig mindsetter to be in. Workers in this group have less security in the long term. Most have skills that are not unique and for which organizations have seasonal needs. People with a gig mindset will be very unhappy in this group because they will struggle with the predefined routine work they are expected to carry out.

## CAUTION AHEAD

The first leaf is getting smaller for many organizations as they move to decrease fixed costs. People in the first leaf must be careful not to fall into the habit of feeling indispensable as part of the core.

In both the first and second leaves, people must focus on their personal development, because both exist in a climate of starting from the top. Will the core needs change? Will you still be part of it? Will your skills still be in demand? Will you be able to move easily from one organization to another? People in the second leaf are more likely to have mobility because they are identified primarily by their skill set and knowledge. People in the first leaf are identified primarily by their organizational affiliation.

Handy's thought-provoking shamrock concept can serve as a simple framework for sensing where you fit inside your organization or in your professional life in general.

# Long-term strategies to start now

## DO YOU WANT TO CRAFT A CAREER OR BUILD VERSATILITY?

As a gig-mindset-oriented person, inside or outside, it is helpful to have a strategy for your work life. I deliberately did not say "strategy for your career." A career in the common sense of the word is only one of your options.

One woman who self-identifies strongly as a gig mindsetter described the way she saw two fundamental choices:

> I see two types of gig-mindset approaches. The first I would describe as a crafting mindset. It's somebody who's choosing

organizations and projects to deliberately craft a career. Then I think there's another kind that I call the versatile mindset. By this, I'm thinking multidiscipline or high curiosity. So, people with this mindset can pursue projects in different areas or disciplines or actually work in several disciplines simultaneously. Versatility is more important to them than a career path.

Imagine two paths: the crafting path and the versatile path. Your choice here will define how you advance inside the organization, and potentially, what your profile will be like if you leave the organization:

- The crafting path, where your goal is to build a career inside the organization, moving up the executive ladder to reach a level where you feel you can have a major influence on the organization and work cultures.

- The versatile path, where you want to develop familiarity and general expertise in different domains, be well connected and widely known throughout the organization, and be able to serve as a bridge between functions, projects, and subgroups.

Both paths can potentially make you part of the professional core, Handy's first leaf, but the crafting path is more likely to lead in that direction. However, each path has advantages and risks.

### THE CRAFTING PATH
- ADVANTAGES:

1. You can build a domain-specific reputation inside the organization, for example in HR or sales, and eventually reach a management level in that domain.

2. Depending on the domain, you can become recognized as a functional expert industry-wide.

3. During a downturn, if you need or decide to move on, you will be marketable in a clearly defined domain.

• RISKS:

1. You may become too attached to an organization.

2. This may lead to a lack of flexibility and a slower ability to adapt in case of a downturn.

**THE VERSATILE PATH**

• ADVANTAGES:

1. You can gain a wide breadth of experience across different domains.

2. It will be easy for you to communicate with people in different areas because you have a broad familiarity with their work.

3. You may become an influencer, a "mover" in your organization because of the number of people you know and have worked with.

• RISKS:

1. You may be perceived as being superficial because you have not developed a deep expertise.

2. In times of restriction or downsizing, the value you bring to the organization will be less visible.

3. People may see you only in your current role and not realize you have other skills and can fulfill other roles.

As a gig mindsetter, you are probably not assembling large numbers of people who work under you. Doing this requires investing time and energy into your "people infrastructure" rather than using your skills and expertise to the benefit of the business. A senior manager based in Canada, with long experience in several enterprises, described how she sees executive development:

It is more difficult to move into senior executive positions as a gig person. Gig mindsetters will have recognition for successful high-profile projects. They are likely to be pretty good at internal networking because they're working with different elements of the organization over time. However, people who excel in the traditional environment spend more time and have more availability to create large organizations underneath them to build up the ways, means, and vision to serve the mission and meet the goals of the company.

The executive network, at this point, still tends to be more traditional in its space. One of the markers of moving to senior leadership is how many people you have reporting to you. So, the executive ladder is pretty clearly defined. People who are more gig-mindset oriented, because they're moving around and their work is more project-centric, aren't amassing large teams or following the traditional markers of an executive promotional ladder.

## A PERSONAL KNOWLEDGE STRATEGY

Whichever path you choose, learning and having a personal knowledge strategy are essential. It makes you more marketable, inside and outside. A high-level manager in a financial institution explained how she saw preparing for the future:

> We're all seeing digital disruption of industry after industry, the rise of artificial intelligence and robots, and [we're] wondering what that means for our jobs. You absolutely must take responsibility for your learning, be a continuous learner, and plan out your future to the extent you can. You absolutely can't wait for somebody to tell you what your career is going to look like. As an employee, you must take ownership. And, yes, lots of people can help you out, but it's entirely up to you to get the learning that you need and make sure that you are making yourself more marketable.

In all cases, you will need to have a structured approach to how you seek out and acquire new knowledge and skills. The seek-sense-share model of personal knowledge mastery developed by Harold Jarche and discussed in Part 4, "Opening Minds and Organizations," shows how people seek and develop new knowledge in networks and connections with others. I invited Jarche to explain it in a simplified format at a networking session I organized in Paris. He described each step:

- Seek: build a network of colleagues, build a network of external people; follow on Twitter or on a feed.

- Sense: think about what you see in your networks, find ways to use it in your work, experiment.

- Share: exchange ideas with others, including your experiments; open yourself to feedback.

Jarche's model has inspired people worldwide. His blog posts are well worth reading for both information and inspiration. His key points reflect a gig mindset, though he does not use that term himself. But the gig mindset does underlie Jarche's approach: awareness (Trait 6), networking (Trait 7), and advancement (Trait 8). (See the full descriptions in Appendix A1.)

### COMMUNITIES WITH EXTERNAL PEOPLE

When I asked leaders in organizations if they are confident they will retain the knowledge and know-how when their people leave, and then looked closely at those organizations that expressed confidence, I saw a correlation between confidence and the makeup of their communities.

The confident segment has a larger proportion of members who are external to the organization. A good example is with communities of interest that bring people together around a topic of shared passion. The confident segment reported that 28 percent of their communities of interest include external people. Among communities that include external people, that is one of the highest proportions I've seen. The more common percentage is from 8 to 15 percent, and rarely 20 percent.

The seventh gig-mindset trait connects individual learning and interacting with others: "I do professional networking extensively, building relationships internally and externally. I actively seek inter-actions with others from whom I learn and to whom I can contribute."

A key concept here is interaction. It is through interactions that we learn. It is not sufficient to learn as individuals. What we observe must be shared and discussed, for it to bring real value.

An experienced consultant in Silicon Valley, who sees herself as gig-mindset oriented, makes networking key in her risk-management strategy:

> Having a network makes you less vulnerable: you develop resil-ience in terms of learning that things are going to shift and change, and if you don't have a network, then you're much more vulner-able and your career could be very brittle and fragile because of that.

We saw earlier that research from the British Standards Insti-tution considers horizon scanning as one of the most important characteristics of resilience. This means being aware of what is hap-pening around us, seeing changes, threats, risks, and opportunities. My own research shows that people with a high gig mindset do more networking—a key part of horizon scanning—than do those with a more traditional mindset. Building strong relations internally and externally helps build resilience in individuals and in organizations.

Whether you are on a crafting path or a versatility path, having a networking strategy and a personal knowledge strategy are impor-tant parts of taking control of your future. Both will help you live the gig-mindset advantage, whether you are inside or outside an organization.

## CASE STUDY: Gig mindset by design

Nishith Desai Associates (NDA) is a small, inventive international law firm that has been recognized by the *Financial Times* as "India's most innovative law firm" for six years and has consistently been in the top five most innovative law firms of the Asia Pacific region. A 31-year-old firm with 120 employees, it has offices in Mumbai, Palo Alto (Silicon Valley), Bangalore, Singapore, New Delhi, Munich, and New York. They provide strategic advice on regulatory, taxation, and other legal matters.

> **The gig mindsetter: Inventive, leaning into the future, ambitious for themselves, their organization, and their customers**
> Gig mindsetters are highly networked, seek out external interactions, and are motivated to develop their skills and knowledge. They learn constantly and share what they learn, internally and externally. They look ahead, explore ideas, and help people in their ecosystem prepare for the future.

"We believe in multiplying 'braincount' over 'headcount.' Stay small, think big, and do big has been our guideline to creating value," explained Nanda Majumdar, leader of Strategy and Transformation. "Our law-firm model is rather contrarian. We embraced the gig mindset starting in 2016 by shifting from a traditional partnership hierarchy to a networked leadership model, based on self-responsibility and self-management." In short, NDA is nonhierarchical, trust-based, and title agnostic.

### FUTURE-ORIENTED FOCUS

NDA stands out from other law firms by providing innovative and strategic advice in future-oriented areas of law such as blockchain and virtual currencies, internet of things (IoT), artificial intelligence, privatization of outer space, drones, robotics, virtual reality, and nanotechnology. They serve Fortune 500 corporations in TMT (technology, media, telecom), financial services, and pharma and healthcare industries.

They not only provide advice to clients in leading-edge areas but demonstrate the same thinking through their own actions. An example is Imaginarium AliGunjan, a research and blue-sky-thinking facility the firm set up in Alibaug, a 45-minute ferry ride from Mumbai. Imaginarium AliGunjan, opened in 2018, is dedicated to encouraging multidisciplinary interactions in philosophy, science, and the arts. NDA describes it as a "modern day pantheon of sorts where world leaders, thinkers and creators converge to design a better future."[4]

### A LAW SCHOOL AFTER LAW SCHOOL

NDA's continuing education program is another example of their preparing for the future. Majumdar said that NDA is often described as a "law school after law school" explaining, "Nearly all law students and lawyers in India use our knowledge site for our 'hotline' [bulletins] and other learning material." NDA has a built-in daily routine for continuing education: every employee is required to do one hour of training every single day.

"We have a virtual learning and working capability built around an easy platform where we can also offer expertise, knowledge, and insights to the external community," she said. "This also lets us bring together the best minds from the outside to make sense of the complex issues that span different domains of law—but even more importantly, how they integrate with larger regulatory, socio-economic-geopolitical issues."

### LEANING TO THE FUTURE WITH CLIENTS

When asked how the pandemic affected NDA's work, Majumdar explained how they extend value to their clients, potential clients, and the larger community (including law students), other professionals like lawyers, accountants, bankers, and so on, through a Client Continuing Education Program, which they called cCep.

The program included a series of online webinars, such as "COVID-19: Force Majeure—Can Parties Renege from Their Contracts?," "How

Do We Accelerate Drone Deliveries during Lockdown?," "How Would Covid-19 Affect Acquiring Distressed Businesses in India?," and "When Surveillance Increases for Safety: How Do We Protect Privacy? How to Play a Balancing Act?"

## INCREASED ENGAGEMENT AND MORALE

I asked Majumdar what impact cCep had on employees. "It has sharpened the competency and intellectual capital, exposure, and confidence of our firm and lawyers," she said. "While webinars, being on panels, and so on, isn't new for our people, the platform to demonstrate their expertise to a vast and diverse audience has been empowering."

She said that it had also lifted engagement, focus, and unity among NDA's people: "The morale and sense of achievement is powerful at a time when job losses, salary cuts, and general distress is overwhelming all around."

I then asked Majumdar what the effect had been on NDA's clients and other external participants. "Many of them are in deep flux and distress," she said. "They have been able to benefit from our expertise and that of people in our network, such as top politicians, bureaucrats, economists, policy makers, investment bankers, venture capitalists, industry experts, entrepreneurs, and domain experts who have been on the cCep panels to offer value."

Majumdar continued: "Our firm's brand as a visible expert has been strengthened and brought confidence to all our stakeholders. We have started doing customized programs for specific clients. 'Client Connect' and 'Law Firm Connect' are two streams we are working on."

## GIG MINDSET, DESIGNED FROM THE INSIDE OUT

"We have decided to work as an 'effectively virtual law firm' on an 80:20 principle, even post-lockdown. Physical presence is meant to be on an as-needed basis, voluntary, and no longer a mandate or norm," Majumdar explained.

The gig mindset started inside, in NDA's work culture, with high autonomy, relentless learning, and a future-oriented focus. It now drives the firm's interactions with the external world. There too the firm empowers people by sharing expertise and helping others get ready for the future, which in many ways is already here. It is not surprising that NDA today is a major contributor to the vast regulatory, industry, policy, and government firmament in India, giving strategic legal, tax, and regulatory advice, relevant today and important for the future.

---

Interview with Nanda Majumdar, leader of Strategy and Transformation at Nishith Desai Associates. www.nishithdesai.com.

# Conclusion
## Living the Gig
## Mindset Advantage

**Uncertainty is the** way of life. It has become normal. We will not move back to an age of stability and certainty in our work lives. We live in volatile times. Our organizations, as well as the world in general, are unlikely to stabilize soon, if ever.

The truth is that our organizations have long been unstable; we just did not see it. Confusion, sometimes chaos, has been building up for a long time as organizations repeatedly restructured, reengineered work practices, and set up change programs—all with the admirable goal of improving business and building resilience for the future. Most of the time, these initiatives did not work, which was why so many companies had to hit reset over and over.

Digital transformation initiatives succeeded in many organizations when they brought new capabilities to employees. But they were primarily focused on technologies and did not bring significant change in how people worked.

The stakes are higher now as organizations and people around the world are forced to create new working conditions in response to the pandemic, which has occurred on top of a host of other global events. We have now been pushed to an extreme of upheavals—internal and external—in how we work. The good side of increasing volatility is that it has both forced and stimulated people to discover new ways of working.

The gig-mindset advantage is part of this. There have been many methods and work models created over the years. The difference with the gig mindset is that it is neither a method nor a model. It is a simple metaphor, quickly grasped, that can be put into action in many ways. You work as if you were a gig worker, but in reality you are a gig mindsetter. Your mental attitude and way of working differ from traditional thinking and behaviors.

We've seen the gig mindset in action in this book through the case studies and examples: focusing on experimentation and sharing failures as well as successes; valuing skills more than roles; working openly and seeking feedback; taking initiatives and assuming responsibility; questioning the status quo; networking internally and externally; following economic, social, and technology trends; and focusing on personal development more than on a career.

We have also looked at the advantages these behaviors bring: building resilience; developing new opportunities; discovering early signs of future trends spotted by people on the edges of the organization; being able to improvise when faced with unexpected events; willingness to take calculated risks when necessary; being able to mobilize the whole organization when faced with a crisis; strengthening the people infrastructure across the organization; having a workforce with new skills; and moving forward with a future-oriented mindset.

## Stories from the future

The companies described in the six case studies are living in the future in different ways. They are examples of values and practices that are an exception today but that will be common in the future, as expressed by a senior manager quoted at the beginning of the book:

Today, people with a gig mindset are the exception, not the rule. But it's like they're early adopters who may well become the rule in the future.

Each organization presented here has found an approach that makes sense for them. Each has found ways to leverage the gig-mindset advantage in their work cultures. Let's take a quick look.

### NEW BEHAVIORS LEADING TO A NEW PRESENT
One company defined a Competency Model based on values and behaviors oriented toward their vision of how they wanted to work. It was not based on goals; it was based on behaviors, many of which underlie the gig mindset. It has lasted for five years.

### LEARNING AND FOCUSING ON THE FUTURE
Another company made learning available and gave people control over what they learned and how. They offered training in future-oriented skills—a proactive strategy, implemented long before the pandemic crisis.

### FROM THE INDIVIDUAL TO THE ORGANIZATION, SHARED LEARNING
And yet another company was also focused on learning and giving people the lead individually. In this case, three specific steps expanded the learning from the individual to the organization through the values of Learn, Apply, Share.

### DESIGNING FLEXIBLE WORK, AND STEPPING OUTSIDE YOUR ROLE
One of the cases focuses on encouraging people to take initiatives outside their official roles and to live and share their interests by including them in work projects.

### LIVING A HEALTHY BALANCE, FLOURISHING BY BLENDING TRADITIONAL- AND GIG-MINDSET WAYS OF WORKING
Another company created a complementary work culture, combining traditional with gig ways of working. Depending on function and time, each way of working helped make the organization stronger.

TAKING THE INSIDE OUT, BUILDING STRENGTH IN THE ECOSYSTEM
One of the companies sought out external interactions, sharing externally what was being learned internally. It is strengthening itself and its ecosystem as it strives to live new ways of thinking and working.

# Pushing boundaries

When we are living the gig-mindset advantage at scale, we will have pushed traditional boundaries. We will have conquered fears and explored new territories. Old lines will have been crossed, creating an expanded vision of the workplace. We will have overcome the artificial boundaries between the group and the individual, between leaders and followers, internal and external, and traditional- and gig-mindset work cultures.

1. **The group versus the individual.** In the past, we focused on the collective group inside the organization, such as "the way we do things here." Relatively recently, we have observed the emergence of the individual, empowered thanks to new digital capabilities. This led us to talk about *me* versus *them* because the boundary between what the person was capable of doing and what was acceptable by the group's traditional practices was solidly in place. In our expanded vision of the workplace, the *I* and *they* will have come together, in a mutually beneficial balance where the individual thrives, as does the organization. We will talk about *us.* We will say "*We* do things in different ways."

2. **Leaders versus followers.** In the past, leadership was a question of hierarchy. Boundaries between high-level decision-makers and the rest of the people were rarely crossed. In our expanded vision of the workplace, we will have realized that leadership is an outcome, not a position. We will have seen multiple failures from misguided leaders and unrealistic, ambitious corporate change programs. We will have also seen cases where ordinary people we had never noticed before achieved great things, such as inventing a new product or service or proposing an idea that changed the marketplace for our business and

the value of the organization. In our expanded vision of the workplace, people from different parts of the organization will be leading through the ways they influence change: they will listen attentively to others, solicit people's opinions from across the organization, and then act. "Top-down" and "bottom-up" are phrases we will no longer hear.

3. **The inside versus the outside.** In the past, the internal organization and the external world were two different spheres. Only exceptionally did internal and external workers collaborate, and then only in carefully controlled online spaces. In our expanded vision of the workplace, these boundaries will have blended to a great extent. We will see that most accomplishments and actions are carried out by mixed teams and groups—internal and external—working as one. In this new operational structure, people will identify themselves and be perceived by others based on their skills and expertise, rather than by which organization they belong to. The distinction between *internal* and *external* worlds will no longer exist. Employees will even move from one to the other and back again as needed. We will talk about the *purpose* of project teams, without referring to their ownership or composition.

4. **The traditional mindset versus the gig mindset.** In the past, work cultures were primarily based on traditional ways of thinking, with doses here and there of the gig mindset. There were clear boundaries between the two styles: experimentation is allowed here but not there; we can question the status quo in a meeting but not when we go back to our real work; leaders want us to feel free to propose ideas but not when they go against established business strategies. Today, in our expanded vision of the workplace, the boundaries will have disappeared. There will be small doses of the traditional mindset but only where it brings value—for example, where it is essential to respect manufacturing processes, follow legal requirements, or carry out management instructions. But even these can be questioned when the timing is right. Overall, workplaces will function with the gig-mindset way of thinking, with high degrees

of autonomy, decentralized decision-making, a focus on skills rather than hierarchy and encouragement to contribute ideas, offering new and sometimes contradictory opinions to the status quo. The term "gig mindset" will no longer be used. Its disappearance proves its success.

Organizations that will have overcome these boundaries will be moving toward self-sustaining resilience, and thereby are more likely to achieve long-lasting success in a fast-changing world.

## Where to start: Structured or spontaneous?

Let's look at three ways to inspire your thinking about where to start. How you implement one or several of these three suggestions depends on whether you decide to work in a structured way or a spontaneous way.

If the first, start with the manifesto (Approach 1), move to the action plan (Approach 2), and then end by selecting action areas (Approach 3). If successful, you will have deployed a widely adopted and self-appropriated evolution to a work culture based on gig-mindset values.

The spontaneous way is useful, powerful in fact, if for political reasons such as reticent management you are not able to work at a visible, strategic level. In this case, start directly with Approach 3 — the items listed in "questions to ask." If successful, this will set off simultaneous individual initiatives throughout the organization that will come together over time to support a more gig-mindset work culture.

1. Define your manifesto, ideally in collaboration with others.

2. Develop an action plan based on goals and finding the appropriate balance between the traditional-mindset and gig-mindset ways of working.

3. Use the lists of "questions to ask" that appear throughout the book and implement the ones relevant for you.

So, let's now look closely at each approach, starting in reverse order:

**Approach 3**: The lists of "questions to ask" are based on themes such as reverse leadership, adaptive capacity, work-life balance, hiring, and performance management. Use them to identify appropriate starting points for yourself, your team, or your organization. You'll find a complete list in Appendix A4, to help you determine the most relevant topics.

**Approach 2**: Developing an action plan is based on the material in Part 6, "Defining a Perpetual Balance." The techniques described will help you conduct a structured analysis and build a decision-making framework collaboratively with others in your organization.

**Approach 1**: Defining a manifesto requires thinking about how you want to live your work life. Doing this with your colleagues, teams, and peers is the best way to ensure appropriation and momentum. The list below offers examples to consider as you think about your own manifesto. As your manifesto is shared with others, the network effect will result in a progressive work culture change, becoming the backbone for future initiatives:

1. Work openly, sharing and seeking feedback.

2. Seek discussion, not consensus.

3. Accept uncertainty, build on it to create greater resilience.

4. Dare to challenge the status quo and to propose alternative approaches.

5. Take initiatives and involve others.

6. Trust and listen to the people on the edges, far from headquarters.

7. Ignore title and positions; focus instead on skills and knowledge.

202 / THE GIG MINDSET ADVANTAGE

8. Follow what's happening in the external world, even in areas that are apparently unrelated to your work today.

9. Make time for learning and for sharing what you learn.

10. Trust yourself, and believe in your capabilities.

To help you build a new perspective, think of your job as temporary, knowing it may disappear tomorrow, and decide how you will prepare for your next context. It may be inside your current organization; it may be elsewhere. Whichever it is, think of it as a new context to develop and not a new job with a title and defined role.

If you manage a team or direct a division or an entire organization, do the same for yourself and the people you are responsible for. Keep in mind that there may be unexpected changes in your industry, in your country, or just in your organizational structure that will impact your role and work.

Living the gig-mindset advantage means focusing and widening your vision simultaneously: focusing on yourself and how you work, and widening your vision to see the big picture. It means cultivating a gig-mindset culture, which is in fact made up of different work cultures, bound together by a belief in the gig-mindset values of initiative, questioning, networking, and openness. This is already underway: your organization, like a few others, probably has a handful of people working like this now. They need to be identified, celebrated, and supported.

This book does not have the answers. No person does. We will make new discoveries together as we advance toward new challenges and opportunities.

# Acknowledgments

GIG MINDSET ADVISORY BOARD

The following were members of the Gig Mindset Advisory Board and I'm grateful for their time commitment, input, and the many discussions we had online as we designed the survey questions.

Adam Cutforth, France; Brian Holness, UK; Catherine Grenfell, Australia; Catherine Shinners, US; Daniel Leonard, the Netherlands; Elena Bogdanova, Russia; Elham Asdaghi, France; Ernst Décsey, Switzerland; Jakob Damsbo, Denmark; Janet Kirkwood, Australia; Jem Janik, US; Kavi Arasu, India; Matt Varney, US; Mike Wagner, US; Nina Sonne Nikolaisen, Denmark; and Sherry McMenemy, Canada.

SURVEY PARTICIPANTS

I would like to acknowledge the 297 people from around the world who participated in the Gig Mindset Survey that took place in 2018. The survey was conducted with an agreement of confidentiality, so I can only thank you as a group. The data collected and your many responses to the open questions were very useful.

PEOPLE INTERVIEWED

Many thanks to the following people, who made time for our hour-long interviews. Many of you spent time thinking about my questions and preparing in advance, and I appreciate that.

Angie Kenechukwu, Nigeria; Anna Ward-Perkins, UK; Brian Holness, UK; Caroline Pickstone, UK; Catherine Shinners, US; Daniel Leonard, the Netherlands; Dave Garrell, UK; Elham Asdaghi, France; Ernst Décsey, Switzerland; Eva Mariana Ramos, Mexico; Heike Roeder, Germany; Janet Kirkwood, Australia; Jem Janik, US; John Turley, UK; Marni Johnson, Canada; Mathieu Rougier, France; Max Bailey, France; Mick Mullane, UK; Nina Sonne Nikolaisen, Denmark; Paul Ward-Perkins, the Netherlands; Sherry McMenemy, Canada; Sue Gemmell, US; and Sylvie Ducamp, France.

PEOPLE WHO HAVE INVESTED TIME AND ENERGY SUPPORTING MY WORK

I greatly appreciated the generous help I received from numerous people around the world. Thank you all for sharing your ideas and giving feedback to mine.

· Jon Husband, Canada, global thought leader, who in 1999 defined the concept of wirearchy, a revolutionary concept for organizations. I've known Jon for many years and am grateful for his constant nudging and stimulating my mind with book references and actionable research by many authors. He helped me define the list in the "Pioneers of the Gig Mindset inside Organizations" section of "Recommended Reading," at the back of this book.

· Indrajit Gupta, India, veteran business journalist, founding editor of *Forbes India*, cofounder of Founding Fuel, which published *The Aadhaar Effect*, about the Indian digital identity project. Indrajit, with long experience in multicultural contexts, offered advice I needed at several critical points in the writing process.

· Kavi Arasu, learning and organization change specialist, principal at Flyntrok and director of Learning and Change at Founding Fuel.

Kavi shared his perspectives on learning and leadership, and was instrumental, along with Indrajit, in introducing people in India to my work.

- Mohammad Hossein Jarrahi, US, associate professor at the University of North Carolina at Chapel Hill. Mohammad generously shared his work on mobile and location-independent knowledge work with me, opening new angles of thought.

- Luis Suarez, Spain, digital transformation and data analytics specialist. Luis was always available for fast, deep feedback when I had questions, needed validations, or was looking for new ideas.

- Harold Jarche, Canada, adviser and international keynote speaker focused on sense-making in networks, communities, and teams. I have had many exchanges with Harold in person and virtually. His blog and workshops on personal knowledge strategies are used by many people around the world.

- Ana Neves, Portugal, founding partner of Knowman, organizer of Social Now. Ana made very useful connections for me, advancing my research, and is one of my thinking partners.

- Thomas Vander Wal, head of Strategy and Planning for DevSecOps and Collaborative Services. Coined the term "folksonomy." Thomas has an amazing in-depth knowledge of many topics and one of the largest networks I know. He responded with specific, detailed background to nearly any inquiry I had.

- Stephen Leybourne, US, Boston University, researcher and author of "Culture and Organizational Improvisation in UK Financial Services," published in *Journal of Service Science and Management* (vol. 2, no. 4). Stephen is one of the few researchers I discovered who has published detailed real cases about improvisation inside organizations.

- Kate Walquist, US, product manager at Upflex, a flexible workspace company. Kate shared her experience about how gig-mindset workers, and corporations as well, are benefiting from coworking spaces.

- Roger Launius, principal at Launius Historical Services. Roger provided information about the Monday Notes, a pioneering example of working out loud, instigated by Wernher von Braun, head of the Marshall Space Flight Center (part of NASA) in the 1960s.

- Christophe Coupez, France, Abalon, specializing in digital transformation for enterprises. Christophe gave me a detailed firsthand view of the life and career of a gig mindsetter inside organizations.

- Valdis Kreb, chief scientist and founder of Orgnet LLC, and a leader in organizational network analysis. Valdis suggested the phrase "stories from the future," which I used in the conclusion, to capture the essence of this book.

- Maish Nichani, Singapore, CEO of PebbleRoad, a design agency integrating information and knowledge strategies.

- Dave Gray, XPLANE founder and author of *The Connected Company, Gamestorming,* and *Liminal Thinking.*

- Subramanian Kalpathi, India, author of *The Millennials: Exploring the World of the Largest Living Generation,* and speaker at Davos 2016.

- Richard Martin, freelance writer and editor, who cast a critical eye over an early draft of the manuscript and gave me valuable preliminary feedback.

CONFERENCES

Special thanks to the conference organizers who have enabled me to test new ideas live with audiences over the years, including the concept of the gig mindset. There's nothing like giving a keynote talk on a new subject and waiting to see how the audience reacts. Will they sit in silence or will they ask questions? In the case of the gig mindset, it was questions—and lots of them.

- Céline Boittin, founder of Céline Boittin Conseil, content and program developer for conferences and events. Organizer of RIRSE in

Paris, where I both chaired and keynoted many years, including specifically about the gig mindset in 2018 and 2019.

- Bjoern Negelmann, longtime organizer of events in Europe exploring the challenges of digital transformation. We have frequently interacted on stage and off about my work and research.

- Kurt Kragh Sørensen, organizer of the European DEX Conference/ IntraTeam Event Copenhagen, where I have keynoted over several years about the organization in the digital age.

- Anastasia Trubnikova, global lead, Employee Experience, HR, and Strategic Intelligence at we.CONECT, who organizes Intra.NET Reloaded, where I gave my first keynote about the gig mindset in 2018.

## WORKSHOPS

A special thanks to two virtual colleagues who organized the worldwide workshops exploring the upsides and downsides of the traditional and gig mindsets. The result of their work is in Appendix A2.

- Catherine Grenfell, community manager, Step Two, in Australia. Catherine led a workshop in Sydney.

- Lau Hesselbæk Andreasen, knowledge broker at ConnectMinds, an international peer-learning and knowledge-sharing network. Lau conducted workshops in Boston, Copenhagen, Edinburgh, Geneva, London, New York, Paris, Philadelphia, Toronto, and Washington, DC.

## MY PUBLISHER

And last but not least, I want to thank the good team at Figure 1 Publishing, who helped me make this book real: Chris Labonté, publisher and president; Tyee Bridge, associate publisher; Lara Smith, managing editor; Jessica Sullivan, creative director; Naomi MacDougall, interior designer; and freelancers Judy Phillips (copy editor), Alison Strobel (proofreader), and Stephen Ullstrom (indexer).

# Appendix A
## The Gig Mindset Research

---

### A1. Traditional-mindset vs. gig-mindset traits

These eight traits for traditional and gig mindsets were defined by me and the research advisory board. They were part of the global survey. The table below has the full descriptions used for the survey. They have been shortened in some cases in this book, but the fundamental meanings are the same.

| TRADITIONAL MINDSET | TRAIT | GIG MINDSET |
|---|---|---|
| I am focused on doing the job while respecting established procedures. I prefer proven and approved methods. | ❶ Motivation | I prefer out-of-the-box thinking and test-and-learn approaches. |
| I feel most comfortable working with people I know, under the leadership of my supervisor, and within the scope of my job role. I like to have a clear definition of roles and responsibilities at all times. | ❷ Roles and Skills | I look for opportunities to work with different types of people in different parts of the organization. I am comfortable with activities and responsibilities defined by skills rather than by roles and hierarchy. |
| I like to progress on a project until an advanced or finished stage before sharing it outside the project team. | ❸ Openness | I am comfortable with opening up early, "working out loud," and taking feedback from outside the project team into account as the project advances. |
| I prefer working under guidance from my supervisor, and with decision-making processes that respect hierarchical flows. | ❹ Autonomy | I prefer to take responsibility for initiating or advancing a project without guidance, and assume responsibility for decisions. |
| Maintaining stability and consistency in how we do things is very important to me. | ❺ Questioning | I often challenge the status quo, including business and work practices. |
| I focus primarily on what is happening inside my organization to feed my thinking and my work. | ❻ Awareness | I am highly aware of what is happening outside my organization that can contribute to my work. I follow what's new in the social, economic, and technology worlds. |
| I tend not to spend time on professional networking, and when I do, it is primarily internal and usually related to the projects I am involved in. | ❼ Networking | I do professional networking extensively, both internally and externally. I actively seek interactions with others from whom I learn and to whom I can contribute. |

| TRADITIONAL MINDSET | TRAIT | GIG MINDSET |
|---|---|---|
| My career path is important to me. My manager and the HR department are key partners to help define my future professional evolution. | ❽ Advancement | My growth path and personal brand are very important to me. I am the one primarily responsible for learning and increasing my knowledge and marketable skills. |

# A2. Upsides and downsides

## BRAINSTORMING ABOUT THE GIG AND TRADITIONAL MINDSETS IN 11 WORKSHOPS AROUND THE WORLD

The following pages contain the results of the 11 workshops conducted around the world. A quick scan will give you an overview of how people inside organizations perceive the two mindsets. If you plan to organize a polarity-navigation exercise in your group, as described in Part 6, "Defining a Perpetual Balance," you will find the details on these pages helpful in preparing for your role as facilitator.

## TRADITIONAL-MINDSET UPSIDES

### WORK CULTURE

- People understand where they belong. The organization is understood. Roles and responsibilities are clear. Faster for people to get up to speed.

- A strong culture that can be more easily mobilized.

- Comfortable for most people, and often the default behavior in a crisis.

- Working with your team, people you know: trust, easy access to information, collaboration.

- Brings stability, security, and protection, which motivates people and increases their loyalty.

### INDIVIDUAL PERSPECTIVE

- Clearer, more structured decision-making can improve accountability. No guesswork as to what my manager expects.

- Standard day: know what needs to be done, do it, then can get out.

- Clearer sense of expertise: who knows what.

### STATUS QUO ACCEPTED

- Little questioning of the strategy, more acceptance.

- Easier to build on lessons learned.

- Seniority prevails. Strong hierarchy. Respect for hierarchy.

- Avoids problem of too many people wanting to be the "chief."

- The majority of salaried people are a base for production for the company. Consistent, constant value. Focus on deployment of a given strategy.

### OPTIMIZATION, EFFICIENCY

- Resources are optimized. With processes in place, employees follow them and can be really effective.

- A certain security in following orders and a predefined road map.

- Better for context where we need efficiency and have simple repetitive tasks and conformity of processes. Good for jobs that require specific results.

- Clear measurements of success and performance/outcomes.

- More focus on the organization than on one's self.

### RISK MANAGEMENT

- Easier to manage risks. Little risk-taking, a comfortable position. Ensures quality for sensitive projects and services.

- Good records/archives of projects/processes.

- Easier to get credit lines from banks.

### CUSTOMER AND BUSINESS BENEFITS

- Reliable for client expectations.

## GIG-MINDSET UPSIDES

### WORK CULTURE

- Learning from sources outside the organization and building an extensive network, more likely to be able to solve problems intuitively and "steal with pride" from others' ideas.

- Work at a faster pace.

- Trying new things; pushing boundaries.

- Quite often would see the bigger picture.

- Focus on outcome, delivery, and value, rather than on the how.

- Agile and able to change course quickly.

- Ability for roles to change to utilize a person's skills.

### INDIVIDUAL PERSPECTIVE

- Feel like I am contributing and a part of something bigger. Become an influencer in an organization—internal and external.

- More fun and agile. You don't know where you'll end up. More fulfilling work. Broadly, more engaging opportunity to "get out of your lane." More freedom and flexibility.

- Opportunities for my career. Gives more responsibility to employees about their own career path (= increased engagement). Meet new people; learn new skills from a broader spectrum of people.

- More cracks to break through and excel. Individual ownership of personal growth.

### SKILLS AND PURPOSE

- Can make more use of people's full skill set.

- Inspire and attract talent. Lower HR costs because self-development is the norm.

- High potential for problem-solving.

- More direct link between skill sets and job role/activities.

- Staff are there because they want to be, not because they are in a "golden cage" of high benefits and salaries.

### LOOKING OUTSIDE

- Future and outward focus of looking at industry-level practices, not just how we do it here.

- Be more reactive to the external environment; capacity to connect with external world to provide innovative solutions.

- Allows creative approaches to work, leading to new opportunities to success and efficiency.

- More flexibility to have roles changed and adapted to suit needs of organization.

### CUSTOMER AND BUSINESS BENEFITS

- Strong capacity of innovation, evolution of products and services, creativity = grow faster.

- Business effective = better and happier employees because they are more empowered.

- Risk-taking can lead to innovation.

## TRADITIONAL-MINDSET DOWNSIDES

### WORK CULTURE

- Management by orders, no or little leadership. "Big Brother is watching you."

- No freedom to innovate, propose, or test new ideas.

- Can be rigid, slow, and restrictive.

- Work takes longer. Progress may be slow.

- Lots of asking for permission.

- When position in hierarchy determines being able to deliver, people must be at a given level to do the work, rather than have the right capability.

- Difficulty to adapt to the external, changing VUCA (volatile, uncertain, complex, and ambiguous) environment.

- Teams are unprepared in case of big change. Not easy to quickly adapt to change.

### PRESENT VS. FUTURE

- Can be insular.

- Can limit thinking, not moving with the times because of rigid and internal focus.

- Can result in work practices to be dated: "That's how we've always done it."

- Miss opportunities to do things better by being stuck in my ways.

- My skills can become obsolete as the world moves on.

- Errors repeated over and over.

### INDIVIDUAL PERSPECTIVE

- Less appealing employer image for young workers.

- Risk of being static: same role, job, team, work.

- Inflexible career paths lead to attrition.

- Boring. Can result in a lack of enthusiasm.

- Can squash personal innovation attempts.

- Redundancy is a more traumatic experience.

### CUSTOMER AND BUSINESS PERSPECTIVE

- Higher risk of final project/service not "usable."

- Will allow competitors to win (red oceans versus blue oceans).

- No or little innovation because of fear of transformation and change is too great.

- We just do what we know and in the same way, even if it doesn't work or is not efficient for people (internal or external).

- Lack of task initiative, or customer-experience improvements: "That's someone else's job."

### SYSTEMS

- Relies on robust systems to be in place from the start.

- Risk averse.

## GIG-MINDSET DOWNSIDES

### UNCERTAINTY

- Testing and learning = too many instances could slow the project and worry leaders.
- Not always obvious what success looks like.
- Problem of stability for quality in mass services. Too much change in general.
- Size of organization needs to be suitable, i.e., difficult for large organizations.

### BLIND SPOTS

- Prone not to include the right people in the process.
- Often do not appreciate the value of other people's roles.

### INDIVIDUAL PERSPECTIVE

- Person can be perceived poorly by hierarchy and colleagues.
- Risk of individualism. Personalities = cult of the individual. Overly focused on personal brand.
- Always on to the next new thing, never finishing anything. Risk of getting involved in too many things and never finishing any of them.
- Longer days, unusual hours. Risk of overcommitment and burnout. "On" all the time.

### CLARITY

- Project responsibilities are left "open to interpretation."

- Difficult to clarify responsibilities and accountability. If someone is underperforming, how is that managed organizationally? Could poor performers "fly under the radar"?
- Can be used as an excuse to cover for bad practices.

### DECISION-MAKING

- Networking: build visions that finally are not well aligned with the company strategy and culture.
- Waste time in collaboration/ aligning on a common view. Difficult to define a strategy.
- Too many meetings and touch points.
- Collective decision-making can end up with too many "leaders" and not enough "doers." Can become "decision by committee."

### KNOWLEDGE

- Higher turnover: difficult long-term planning.
- Loss of corporate knowledge and the why and how of the way things are done.

### CUSTOMER AND BUSINESS PERSPECTIVE

- Neglect of business as usual which becomes unattractive and boring.
- Difficult to manage if the leader is of a traditional mindset.
- People willing to take risks when maybe they shouldn't.

## A3. Functions, job roles, and mindsets

WHICH MINDSET BEST SUITS PARTICULAR ROLES,
JOBS, OR PROJECTS?

| Traditional mindset | | Gig mindset | |
|---|---|---|---|
| Finance, procurement | HR: Compensations, Benefits, mobility | CEO, board | Help desk |
| Audit | | Business, sales | |
| Accounting | Lawyers, legal | Business intelligence | |
| Cost control | Administrative assistants | Project leaders | |
| Regulatory affairs | | | |
| Health & safety | Customer-support teams | Organizational | Marketing |
| Back office | | IT, operations | Digital manager |
| Supply chain | | Marketing | Communication |
| Product | | Advertising | HR |
| Quality control | | CTO | Happiness officer |
| | | Sales teams | |
| Project manager for large projects | | R&D Innovation | Transformation & change teams |
| CTO and IT, system- or process-driven jobs | | | |

### Types of organizations

| | | | |
|---|---|---|---|
| Civil servants | *Businesses where taking risks is dangerous, i.e., nuclear industries.* | Teachers | *Finance jobs i.e., projects involving lots of risk-taking such as traders.* |
| Mass repetitive products | | Developers | |
| Army | | Creative arts | |
| Healthcare professionals | | Graphic designers | |
| Banking | | Artists & designers | |
| Factory jobs | | Event managers | |
| Large groups/ companies | | Startups | |

A second dimension explored in workshop mode was to see if there are specific roles or functions in the organization better suited to either the gig or the traditional mindset.

The responses to this question led us to several observations:

#### AMBIDEXTERITY IN MANY FUNCTIONS

- There are support jobs and roles on both sides—HR and IT, for example. This shows us that functional roles can be carried out in traditional ways or gig-mindset ways. One person felt that "all support functions to make things change" (IT, HR, Finance) are on the gig side. This is a relatively new perspective as these functions tended to be traditional in their work approach in the past.

- Service to customers is also on both sides: customer support teams on the traditional side and help desk on the gig side. This needs to be examined closer to see if the difference depends on the industry involved, the company culture, or the people themselves.

- Risk is perceived to be relevant to both mindsets. Notice that under "types of organization," the nuclear industry is placed under traditional and financial traders under gig. Perhaps because one is physical risk and the other "just" financial?

These three points are worth exploring in a future research initiative. It is important to understand how people perceive job functions on the gig-traditional spectrum. A dimension to explore is to determine whether people are influenced by how the functions worked in the past or whether they have rethought how these functions could or should operate in the future. For example, IT was long considered the traditional, inflexible guardian of workplace technologies. Today, many IT people are of the gig mindset, leading experiments in new tools and self-controlled solutions. HR, long the enforcer of rigid policies and procedures for hiring and performance reviews, is another example. Numerous HR practitioners are now thinking outside the box and practicing new methods, such as socialized performance management using ongoing communication and feedback.

## A4. Questions to think about

Below is a list of the 14 short sets of questions included in the book. They are useful to consider when you are thinking about the work culture in your organization and your own mindset. They offer good points for kicking off discussion in a team meeting or workshop. You can also use all 14 to build a workshop agenda around the gig-mindset work culture and how to stimulate and cultivate it in your organization.

The full list is provided here to make it easier for you to find them when you need them.

PART 1: WHAT IS THE GIG MINDSET?
- You, the individual
- You, the senior leader

PART 2: THE FUTURE IS AT STAKE
- Willful blindness and external awareness

PART 3: BUILDING PROACTIVE RESILIENCE
- Adaptive capacity
- Reachability

PART 4: OPENING MINDS AND ORGANIZATIONS
- Reverse leadership
- Defining fundamental principles
- Decentralized decision-making
- Openness across your organization
- Improvisation
- Work-life balance
- Collaboration

PART 5: INVESTING IN THE MOVERS
- Hiring in the gig-mindset age
- Performance evaluation

# A5. The Gig Mindset Survey

## SURVEY PARTICIPANTS

You can see the number of participants per country at this page on my website: www.netjmc.com/global-scale-for-the-gig-mindset-research-2018/.

Forty-nine percent were from Europe, 25 percent from Asia, 19 percent from North America, and 6 percent from Oceania, which includes Australia.

## SURVEY QUESTIONS

Part 1, "Working Styles," was identical to the questions in the Mindset Profiler, which you can find in Part 6, Step 1.

People were asked to look at the eight traits describing the traditional mindset and the gig mindset. They were given the list you see in the table in the section "Traditional-Mindset vs. Gig-Mindset Traits," in Appendix A1.

They were told to think about where they felt the most comfortable, and to score themselves on a scale from 1 (highly traditional mindset) to 5 (highly gig mindset). They were reminded that it is normal to feel they are not at either extreme, and that they probably fall somewhere between the 1 and the 5, so should not hesitate to mark a 2, 3, or 4.

Part 2, "Work Cultures and Practices in Your Organization," covered the organizational aspects. Participants were asked to rate the following items on a 5-degree scale, where 1 = "strongly disagree" and 5 = "strongly agree."

## WORK CULTURE

- We have a strong, shared sense of organizational purpose and identity.

- We practice decentralized decision-making, down to the lowest level of accountability.

- People are encouraged to experiment and take initiatives.

- We have a culture of rewarding people for problem-solving.

- People are able to learn and develop their skills and knowledge as a natural part of working.

### FLEXIBILITY

- Our organization can respond rapidly to major events or transitions: market changes, competition, economic downturns, environmental or disaster events.

### HOW PEOPLE AND TEAMS WORK

- In general, people self-manage and self-direct their work within the generally established processes as they see best.

- We have many distributed, cross-functional teams, where people work together across silos.

- Teams willingly make their work visible to the larger organization as they work, and before the work is finished. They work out loud through ongoing use of internal social and communication channels.

- Teams are empowered to act, and they feel safe reinventing how they work, including shortcutting enterprise processes in order to advance rapidly.

### OPEN COMMUNICATION

- Business goals and plans are openly communicated throughout the organization.

- People are encouraged to give input to business goals and plans, and to challenge ideas, including our business model and work practices.

- Overall, our senior leaders have an open and participatory style, and are willing to listen to and consider input from people when making decisions.

### TALENT AND SKILLS

*Multichoice list to tick. Multiple responses possible.*

- It is possible to solicit people for projects based on their skills and not just on their roles. (For example, the skill of "data extraction techniques" versus the role of "data migration lead.")

- We are able to do a talent inventory to see what expertise and skills we have in our organization today.

- We have an internal talent marketplace where people can "advertise" their experience/skills/expertise, and project leaders can describe their needs for project teams.

- We use external talent marketplaces when we need talent/skills that we do not have internally.

#### CHALLENGES AND THE FUTURE
*Participants gave their assessments on a scale of 1 to 5, where 1 = "very slow" and 5 = "very fast."*

- Pace of change inside: How would you rate the pace of change and transformation overall in your organization (e.g., business, digital, structural, cultural)?

- Pace of change in your sector: How would you rate the pace of change and transformation in your sector or area of activity (e.g., business, digital, political, cultural)?

*In the following questions, participants responded using these options: Yes, Possibly, No, Don't know, or N/A (not applicable).*

**Organizational impact:** Has the gig mindset had an impact on your organization?

Reminder: the gig mindset refers to attitudes and behaviors of people who, even though they are salaried employees in an organization, approach their work more as if they were independent freelancers.

**Personal impact:** Has the gig mindset had an impact on the way you personally work?

**Work-life balance:** Do you think that people working with more of a gig mindset and attitude find it hard to keep a healthy work-life balance (potentially risking burnouts)?

**Gig mindset pockets:** Is there a part of your organization that is working with or leaning toward the gig mindset today (e.g., business unit, function, department)?

*Open question:*

**Encourage or discourage:** How does your organization encourage or discourage the gig-mindset way of working? Can you share some examples?

### DEMOGRAPHIC QUESTIONS

*A series of demographic information was requested to analyze the data.*

**Organization:** type, size of workforce, age of organization, sector(s) of activity, global presence.

**The person responding:** department or function, level and role, age range, seniority in the organization. The person's name and organizational affiliation were not obligatory questions. Some answered, others did not.

## A6. Case studies

Below, the six case studies presented in the book are listed by theme. The case studies can be found at the end of each part.

### PART 2. THE FUTURE IS AT STAKE

#### BEHAVIORS THAT TRANSFORM

Merck KGaA, Darmstadt, Germany, is a science and technology company operating in the healthcare, life science, and performance-material sectors, with some fifty-seven thousand people in 66 countries.

They have developed a future-oriented Competency Model as a framework to guide processes and decision-making across the organization. This model, in place since 2015, is highly structured yet simple, a framework that encourages, validates, and rewards many gig-mindset behaviors and offers a foundation for a stimulating work culture.

## PART 3: BUILDING PROACTIVE RESILIENCE

#ILOVELEARNING AT AIR LIQUIDE

Air Liquide is an international company with a presence in 80 countries. Founded in 1902, it has a long tradition of innovation. With sixty-seven thousand employees worldwide, it specializes in gases, technologies, and services for industry and the health sector.

Air Liquide developed a self-learning program and a virtual campus. They were proactive in making learning opportunities available to people and giving them control over what they learn and how. This approach is likely to keep gig mindsetters motivated to do their best work for the organization.

## PART 4: OPENING MINDS AND ORGANIZATIONS

SHIFT AT SANOFI

Sanofi is a diversified global healthcare company, operating in over 170 countries and providing a range of healthcare solutions to individuals. It consists of three core global business units: Specialty Care, Vaccines, and General Medicines. Consumer Healthcare is a stand-alone business unit.

Sanofi has developed an original learning strategy based on three principles: Learn, Apply, Share. It starts with the person and finishes with the organization. This is a powerful way to blend the ambitions of gig-mindset-oriented people to the ambitions of the organization.

## PART 5: INVESTING IN THE MOVERS

VELCRO MANAGEMENT IN ACTION

BlueShore Financial, based in Vancouver, Canada, offers a range of services in banking, borrowing, wealth management, insurance, and business solutions. The company has 370 employees and has won numerous awards for its work culture.

A gig-mindset work culture strengthens organizations because it encourages people to go beyond their official job role, to share and live their interests. This builds a strong, flexible, and passionate human infrastructure in the organization. This is the essence of Velcro management and a fundamental part of the gig-mindset work culture.

## PART 6: DEFINING A PERPETUAL BALANCE
### ENTREPRENEURSHIP IN A BIMODAL WORK CULTURE

A global agricultural commodity trading company (referred to as ACTC to respect its request for anonymity) works in a bimodal culture.

The gig mindset and the traditional mindset are polarities: interdependent and complementary. Whereas most organizations have insufficient gig-mindset behaviors, ACTC has found the right balance. The teams that work in gig-mindset mode rely on those that represent a traditional way of working, and vice versa. Together, they flourish.

## PART 7: OWNING YOUR PERSONAL STRATEGY
### GIG MINDSET BY DESIGN

Nishith Desai Associates (NDA) is a small, inventive international law firm that has been recognized by the *Financial Times* as "India's most innovative law firm" for six years and has consistently been in the list of top five innovative law firms in the Asia Pacific region.

The people in Nishith Desai Associates are highly networked, seek out external interactions, and are motivated to develop their skills and knowledge. They learn constantly and share what they learn, internally and externally. They look ahead, explore ideas, and help people in their ecosystem prepare for the future.

# Appendix B
## Evolution of the Workplace

### B1. A 20-year, four-phase perspective

The following table shows the big picture of how the workplace has evolved over the past 20 years. It shows the correlations between the digital work environment and the mindset of the organization.

#### PHASE 1: TOP-DOWN, ONE-WAY FLOWS OF CAREFULLY CRAFTED INFORMATION

PASSIVITY RULES. POWER IN THE HANDS OF HQ AND COMMUNICATION DEPARTMENTS.

Phase 1, the authoritative top-down environment from 20 years ago, was the starting point for most organizations. In the early 2000s, internal digital work environments—intranets, as they were then called—functioned with centralized publishing and were top-down, HQ-driven, and designed for the office-based workforces. Departments and central functions used the intranet to publish information about themselves and the services they offered employees.

## The digital work environment and the mindset of the organization are inextricably linked: A 20-year perspective

| | THE DIGITAL WORK ENVIRONMENT | THE MINDSET OF THE ORGANIZATION |
|---|---|---|
| Authoritative, stable, managed dimension | PHASE 1. Managed information and enterprise applications. Structured by function, with distinct "territories," the goal is to inform. | The traditional mindset underlies this phase. Hierarchy rules and the flows are nearly exclusively top-down. There is a strong sense of territory. |
| Authoritative, stable, managed dimension — Structured collaboration dimension | PHASE 2. Structured project collaboration brings "real work" to the digital environment. Goals become productivity and efficiency. | The traditional mindset is still strong, although project teams are empowered. However, project work is rarely visible to people outside the projects. |
| Social collaboration dimension — Authoritative, stable, managed dimension — Structured collaboration dimension | PHASE 3. Social media disrupts, empowering people in theory, giving them voice, but stays in its own corner, isolated from "real work." | The gig mindset is appearing, though with little visibility across the organization. Gig-mindset behaviors not yet integrated into work and projects. |
| + Mobile dimension | PHASE 4. The three spaces blend, with social bringing visibility and openness for individuals and teams. Mobile devices give people choice and freedom as to where they work. | The technologies and terrain are conducive to the gig mindset. It is emerging slowly in many organizations. *However, the leadership mindset is not yet ready.* |

Remnants of it still exist in many digital work environments. This mirrors the management culture in organizations where command-and-control leadership is still predominant and the gig mindset is practically nonexistent.

## PHASE 2: TIMID SIGNS OF INTERACTIVITY, BUSINESS SUPPORT, AND MOBILE

EYES ARE OPENING. THE SLOW AWAKENING OF PEOPLE TO THE POWER OF PEOPLE-GENERATED CONTENT AND NETWORKING.

Phase 2 reflects the moment in time when business managers got involved in doing project work collaboratively online. Technology played a role here by making it possible to create closed digital spaces for teams. Politics and power games started at this point, as business managers and communication managers each wanted their own digital space to be employees' entry point into the digital workplace. The gig mindset had not yet emerged, as this phase was highly siloed into departments, functions, and teams.

## PHASE 3: BOTTOM-UP LIBERATION MOVEMENTS

POWER TO THE PEOPLE. SELF-DIRECTION BORN, BUT NOT YET EVERYWHERE.

Phase 3 was the beginning of bottom-up initiatives creating spontaneous movements where organizational leaders began to experience a loss of control. It was powered by individuals' needs for things the organization was not providing. Three movements were based on technologies that liberated people:

- Isolated social media tools, such as unofficial wikis and blogs, were used inside organizations. Although at first counter to IT guidelines, they were slowly replaced by official enterprise social networks.

- The unauthorized, potentially risky use of consumer cloud services started to become part of official enterprise cloud solutions.

- Use of one's personal mobile device (BYOD, or bring your own device), which started with people at the edges of organizations serving customers, was transformed into use of corporate devices and creative technology solutions that made personal devices secure.[1]

Here we see the potential for the gig mindset coming to life: people sharing their thoughts and information with others and starting interactions with questions, comments, and conversation. Some organizations created simple social networks but usually kept them separate from business conversations, marketing and sales work, and so on—what they considered to be "real work."

### PHASE 4: THE HERE-AND-NOW ERA
ME AND THE PEOPLE I WORK WITH—INSIDE AND OUTSIDE.

Phase 4 was the start of a collaborative digital work environment, what some refer to as Enterprise 2.0, and was the moment when gig-mindset behaviors were starting in a few people. Authoritative enterprise information and systems began to blend with project and structured collaboration, which in turn connected to the social-collaboration dimension. A higher degree of personalization was starting. This was a turning point, in that senior management got seriously involved. The external world began to enter via virtual communities and project spaces with external people.

The transition from phase 3 to phase 4 was gradual and influenced primarily by the increasing number of mobile devices people were using in the workplace. This let people access collaboration spaces directly and interact with colleagues—all without ever passing by that prize real estate, the homepage. Companies began to offer news feeds, apps, and ways that people could build their own entry points. Corporate strategies varied greatly, from imposing minimal content on the entry point to imposing most of the content. Whichever strategy was deployed, people had much more freedom and many more choices than previously. The potential of the gig mindset inside the organization is now clearly mirrored by the digital work environment.

In my descriptions of the four phases, I repeatedly use the word "potential" when referring to the gig mindset. This is because the digital work environment no longer blocks the gig mindset, which is far from saying it encourages it. It enables it, potentially, and a slowly increasing number of people are manifesting the behaviors to a lesser or greater degree.

## B2. Ten years of research on the organization in the digital age

My web page "About the Research Participants" presents the profiles of the participants in my research of the organization in the digital age. It gives types of organizations, size, countries, marketing positioning, sectors of activity, and an overview of the age of organizations—some over two hundred years old—and their digital maturity. www.netjmc.com/about-the-research/

## B3. The Foundational Framework for the Organization in the Digital Age

In 2013, I created the Foundational Framework for the Organization in the Digital Age. It was one of the first attempts in the industry to build a framework bringing together people, technology, and the organization. It is organized in nine dimensions, grouped as Mindset, Enablers, and Capabilities. Over one hundred data points gathered through self-assessment by survey participants served different purposes: a snapshot of a given organization in the digital age, comparisons among industry sectors, and an overview of evolution from 2014 through 2016, three formative years for *digital inside* organizations.

The data I gathered over this period alerted me to the emergence of the individual dimension: creating, sharing, learning, and growing.

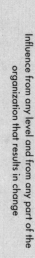

Managing the digital work environment as a strategic asset, essential for the organization

Creating, sharing, learning, and growing

Serving clients, customers, or users of the organization's services and products

Cross-organizational perspective: working across silos as a networked organization

Influence from any level and from any part of the organization that results in change

INDIVIDUAL

CUSTOMER

ENTERPRISE

ASSET

LEADERSHIP

MINDSET

CULTURE

PROCESS

STRUCTURE

REACH

CAPABILITIES

ENABLERS

PEOPLE

TECH-NOLOGY

WORK-PLACE

Attitudes, behaviors, styles, and expectations in ways of working

New and simplified processes that reflect social collaborative ways of working

Virtual operational units, such as communities and networks, complementing hierarchical structures

Equal, relevant, interactive digital access for the entire workforce, connecting people anywhere, anytime

Here is a short summary of each dimension (moving in a counter-clockwise manner):

### CAPABILITIES

- **Individual:** Creating, sharing, learning, and growing.

- **Customer:** Serving clients, customers, or users of the organization's services and products.

- **Enterprise:** Cross-organizational perspective: working across silos as a networked organization.

### ENABLERS

- **Reach:** Equal, relevant, interactive digital access for the entire workforce. Connecting everyone anywhere, anytime.

- **Structure:** Virtual operational units, such as communities, teams, and networks, complementing hierarchical structures.

- **Process:** New and simplified processes to reflect social collaborative ways of working.

### MINDSET

- **Culture:** Attitudes, behaviors, styles, and expectations in ways of working.

- **Leadership:** Influence from any level and from any part of the organization that results in change.

- **Asset:** Managing the digital work environment as a strategic asset, essential for the organization.

You'll find the list of data points for each of the nine dimensions on my web page "9 Dimensions," at www.netjmc.com/9-dimensions-of-the-organization-in-the-digital-age/.

## B4. Emergence of the individual

The chart below traces the evolution of the nine dimensions of the Foundational Framework for the Organization in the Digital Age over three consecutive years of research. Individual grew the most, with a 40% increase, and became the strongest dimension of the nine.

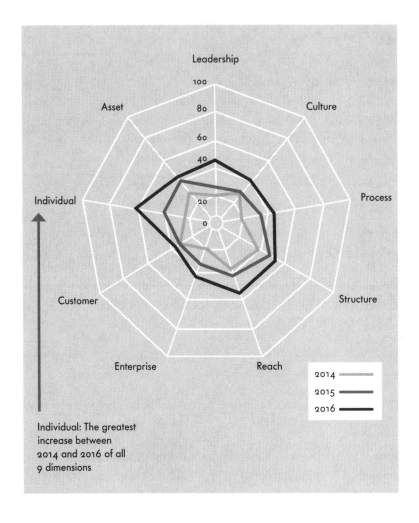

Individual: The greatest increase between 2014 and 2016 of all 9 dimensions

## B5. Organizational capabilities tracked over three years

Four organizational capabilities were self-assessed by survey participants in three consecutive annual surveys from 2014 through 2016.
There was a minimum of three hundred participants from around the
world each year. They were asked to answer four questions about key
capabilities in their organization as whole. There were five degrees of
answer options, ranging from "very" to "not at all."

1. How easy is it for people to learn and develop their skills and
   knowledge in the natural flow of work? (Replies of "very easy" and
   "relatively easy" grew from 40 percent in 2014 to 53 percent in 2016.)

   - People learning as they work showed the most progress over
     the three-year period. This was an important data point used
     to detect the emergence of the gig mindset. In Part 4, "Opening
     Minds and Organizations," you read about the importance of fast
     learning. Although we looked at a three-year period from 2014
     to 2016 in this comparison of four organizational capacities, if we
     take a larger span on the "people learning" point, we see an even
     greater growth, from 23 percent in 2013 to 66 percent in 2018.

2. How easy is it for customer-facing people to find the information they
   need, provide rapid service, collaborate with their customers and
   colleagues, and in general have a smooth and efficient work experience? (The "very easy" and "relatively easy" numbers grew from
   33 percent to 39 percent in the three-year period, much less growth
   than "people learning.")

   - Customer-facing people have long been the losers when it comes
     to access to organizational information and knowledge. This has
     often made them adopt gig-mindset behaviors, acting creatively
     to meet their needs. In Part 4, "Opening Minds and Organiza-
     tions," we talked about accountable decentralization, and the
     need to trust the edges in order to stay in touch with what is
     happening.

3. How flexible is your organization when you need to react rapidly to major events: market changes, new competition, economic downturns, environmental or disaster events? (Here, the increase for "very flexible" and "relatively flexible," from 26 percent to 30 percent in the same period, is even lower.)

   • Most organizations are not very flexible, as we saw in Part 3, "Building Proactive Resilience," specifically in the section on adaptive capacity and how it is the counterpoint to horizon scanning. The people on the edges may detect change, but it will serve little purpose if the organization cannot adapt accordingly.

4. How confident are you that your organization can retain the knowledge and know-how of experts and specialists when they leave the organization? (This capacity, the lowest of the four, stagnated at 13 percent between 2014 and 2016 for "very confident" and "relatively confident.")

   • As discussed in Part 4, "Opening Minds and Organizations," continuous interactions among people, networking internally and externally, and sharing with others are important ways to use, retain, and develop knowledge. Working out loud—sharing work before it is finished, to get input from others—is also an important practice that is not yet widespread. The sections "Continuous and Connected, Internally and Externally" and "Openness and Working Out Loud" develop these points.

# Recommended Reading

**PIONEERS OF THE GIG MINDSET INSIDE ORGANIZATIONS**
Although "gig mindset" as a term did not yet exist, the following researchers and authors explored and worked on ideas and concepts that are closely aligned. They provide a diverse sense-making framework well worth discovering. This is not an exhaustive list but a good starting point for readers interested in exploring early, innovative organizational thinking.

The books listed below can be found in bookstores, libraries, and online sources. I have listed websites for the concepts for which there is no specific book.

1960. Douglas McGregor, *The Human Side of Enterprise*, McGraw-Hill. This is considered to be one of the most important management books ever written and has influenced many organizational thinkers since. McGregor distinguishes between two theories about people: theory Y–individuals are self-motivated and self-directed and theory X–employees must be commanded and controlled by managers. The two theories underlie much thinking, discussion, and management practices up to today.

1977. Albert Bandura, "Self-Efficacy: Toward a Unifying Theory of Behavioral Change," *Psychological Review*, vol. 84, no. 2, pp. 191-215. dradamvolungis.files.wordpress.com/2011/06/self-efficacy-unifying-theory-of-behavioral-change-bandura-1977.pdf. About Bandura's concept of self-efficacy.

1985. Gifford Pinchot, *Intrapreneuring: Why You Don't Have to Leave the Corporation to Become an Entrepreneur*, Harper & Row.

1989. Charles Handy, *The Age of Unreason*, Harvard Business School Press. A forward-looking book of its time, discussing discontinuous change, the disappearance of lifelong jobs, and the need for upside-down thinking.

1990. Peter Senge, *The Fifth Discipline: The Art and Practice of the Learning Organization*, Cornerstone Digital. His thesis is that the only sustainable competitive advantage for organizations is their ability to learn.

1996. Art Kleiner, *The Age of Heretics: Heroes, Outlaws, and the Forerunners of Corporate Change*, 1st ed., Jossey-Bass. Heretics as visionaries able to create change inside organizations.

1997. Gareth Morgan, *Imaginization: New Mindsets for Seeing, Organizing, and Managing*, SAGE; Berrett-Koehler. The end of organized organizations and the era where self-organization is a key competence.

1999. Darcy DiNucci coins the term "Web 2.0," meaning the participatory or social web. Interestingly, Tim Berners-Lee, creator of the Web protocol "http" said in 2006 that the original vision of Web 1.0 was "all about connecting people. It was an interactive space, and I think Web 2.0 is of course a piece of jargon, nobody even knows what it means. If Web 2.0 for you is blogs and wikis, then that is people to people. But that was what the Web was supposed to be all along."[1]

1999. Jon Husband coins the term "wirearchy," which he defines as the organizing principle for an era of interconnected knowledge, trust, and credibility. Husband edited the collective work *Wirearchy: Sketches for the Future of Work*. wirearchy.com.

1999. Rick Levine, Christopher Locke, Doc Searls, and David Weinberger, *The Cluetrain Manifesto: The End of Business as Usual*, Basic Books. Dedicated to the topic of marketing in the internet age, the book is also relevant to what happens inside organizations, with sections such as "Hyperlinks Subvert Hierarchy" and "Intranets and the Impact to Organization Control and Structure."

1999. Peter Cappelli, *The New Deal at Work: Managing the Market-Driven Workforce*, Harvard Business School Press. Cappelli explores the profound change in the relationship between employees and employers.

2004. Thomas Vander Wal coins the term "folksonomy" to describe a system of collaborative tagging and classification combining the ideas of taxonomy and folk. This was part of giving people a means to define their own systems of classification to supplement the official systems, or to use when no official system existed. The term is not well known outside the consultant and tech world, but it is a key part of the gig-mindset culture: giving people control of how they organize information. vanderwal.net/folksonomy.html.

## ABOUT RESILIENCE

What follows is a nonexhaustive list of academic and management thinkers who have researched and defined resilience. This list was a helpful source for my thinking about resilience as it relates to the gig mindset. It also includes other books and articles you may find relevant for digging deeper into the topic.

The subject of how the gig mindset strengthens resilience is developed in Part 3, "Building Proactive Resilience."

### BUSINESS AND MANAGEMENT WRITERS

1997. Arie de Geus, *The Living Company: Habits for Survival in a Turbulent Business Environment*, Harvard Business School Press. Based on a study carried out when de Geus was at Royal Dutch Shell to identify shared criteria in the longest-living large companies.

2003. Gary Hamel and Liisa Välikangas, "The Quest for Resilience," *Harvard Business Review*, September.

## SCIENTISTS

2006. Brian Walker and David Salt, *Resilience Thinking: Sustaining Ecosystems and People in a Changing World*, Island Press.

2010. Carl Folke, Stephen R. Carpenter, Brian Walker, Marten Scheffer, Terry Chapin, and Johan Rockström, "Resilience Thinking: Integrating Resilience, Adaptability and Transformability," *Ecology and Society*, vol. 15, no. 4, art. 20 (online), www.ecologyandsociety.org/vol15/iss4/art20/.

## ORGANIZATIONAL THEORISTS: KARL WEICK AND ASSOCIATED RESEARCHERS AND WRITERS

Karl E. Weick, *Making Sense of the Organization*, vol. 2: *The Impermanent Organization*, John Wiley & Sons, 2009.

Karl Weick and Kathleen M. Sutcliffe's *Managing the Unexpected: Sustained Performance in a Complex World* was published in its third edition in 2015. The first edition, *Managing the Unexpected: Assuring High Performance in an Age of Complexity*, dates from 2001 (Jossey-Bass). The second edition, *Managing the Unexpected: Resilient Performance in an Age of Uncertainty*, is from 2007 (Jossey-Bass).

Karl Weick, Kathleen Sutcliffe, and David Obstfeld, "Organizing for High Reliability: Processes of Collective Mindfulness," published in 1999 as a section in *Research in Organizational Behavior*, vol. 1, JAI Press, pp. 81–123. This work is a rather dense, academic approach to the topic. However, it highlights processes that build collective mindfulness, which in turn leads to the ability to discover and manage unexpected events.

## INSURANCE INDUSTRY STUDIES

Two studies were done for Airmic, a not-for-profit UK-based organization created in 1963, to promote the interests of corporate insurance buyers and those involved in enterprise risk management, and to encourage best practice. The first study, *Roads to Ruin: A Study of Major Risk Events: Their Origins, Impact and Implications* (2011), conducted by Cass Business School, analyzes 18 major corporate crises, some leading to the disappearance of the company, others leading to major damage.

The analysis includes the ecosystems of the companies and references a total of 40 organizations.

Although the study does not develop the concept of the gig mindset, many of the findings correspond effectively to a gig mindset, or rather, the lack of one. Examples include leadership ego, glass ceilings at high levels (preventing internal teams from reporting on risks), board-level risk blindness, excessive complexity, lack of awareness of new trends and technologies, lack of a moral compass, and severe lack of communication between frontline workers and management.

The second study, *Roads to Resilience: Building Dynamic Approaches to Risk* (2014), carried out by Cranfield School of Management, is based on in-depth case studies of eight companies that showed resilience in contexts where things went well but could have turned out badly.

You can find the studies at www.airmic.com/technical/library and then using the search function.

## ABOUT IMPROVISATION

The subject of improvisation has fascinated academics for years. The gig mindset is highly conducive to improvisation, giving organizations with a gig-mindset-friendly culture one foot up in our fast-changing world of unexpected, sudden events.

The sources I have drawn on include the following works. This list includes works not referred to in this book. I recommend you take a look at them individually if you want to deepen your understanding of organizational improvisation. Although there are few published case studies as of this writing, it is developing as a field of study.

### OVERVIEWS

2003. "Organizational Improvisation: What, When, How and Why," an article written by Miguel Pina e Cunha, João Vieira da Cunha, and Ken Kamoche and published in *International Journal of Management Reviews*, vol. 1, no. 3, pp. 299–341, is a detailed overview of the research carried out as of that time. They have numerous references that can be sought out, with the books usually available only in hardback. One in particular is "Organizing for Innovation," by D. Dougherty (1996), which appeared in *Handbook of Organization Studies*, by S.R. Clegg, C. Hardy, and W.R. Nord (eds.), SAGE, pp. 424-39.

2009. *Making Sense of the Organization*, vol 2: *The Impermanent Organization*, by Karl E. Weick, John Wiley & Sons.

2012. *Yes to the Mess: Surprising Leadership Lessons from Jazz*, by Frank J. Barrett, Harvard Business Review Press.

2014. "Organizational Improvisation: A Consolidating Review and Framework," by Allègre L. Hadida, William Tarvainen, and Jed Rose. Available in free access at doi.org/10.1111/ijmr.12047 (accessed August 22, 2020). This paper offers a detailed overview of research about organizational improvisation, with several useful frameworks and summaries of terms used by different researchers.

2019. "Improvisation in the Learning Organization: A Defense of the Infra-Ordinary." Miguel Pina e Cunha and Stewart Clegg go into the everyday dimension of improvisation in their article; www.research gate.net/publication/330379217_Improvisation_in_the_learning_ organization_a_defense_of_the_infra-ordinary (accessed August 3, 2020).

**SPECIFIC DIMENSIONS OF IMPROVISATION**
1996. "Swift Trust and Temporary Groups," by Debra Meyerson, Karl E. Weick, and Roderick M. Kramer, in *Trust in Organizations: Frontiers of Theory and Research* by Roderick M. Kramer and Tom R. Tyler (SAGE, 1996, pp. 166-95). Accessed August 22, 2020, at doi.org/10.4135/ 9781452243610.n9.

2001. "Organizational Improvisation and Learning: A Field Study," by Anne S. Miner, Paula Bassof, and Christine Moorman, published by SAGE on behalf of the Samuel Curtis Johnson Graduate School of Management, Cornell University. Two case studies are developed, one a software company and the other a retail food company. Paywall. Accessed August 22, 2020, at journals.sagepub.com/doi/abs/10.2307/2667089.

# Endnotes

**PREFACE: BECOMING AWARE**
1  The Gig Mindset Advisory Board 2018 is presented on my web page of the
   same name. There, you can also click through to each member's LinkedIn
   profile. www.netjmc.com/gig-mindset-advisory-board-2018/.
2  My web page "About the Research Participants" presents the profiles of
   the participants in my research of the organization in the digital age. It
   shows the global spread, types of organizations, size, countries, marketing
   positioning, sectors of activity, and an overview of the age of organizations—
   some over two hundred years—and their digital maturity. www.netjmc.com/
   about-the-research/.

**PART 1: WHAT IS THE GIG MINDSET?**
1  You can do the full survey by using the document in Appendix A5. The
   questions cover both individual behaviors and work practices.
2  Many organizational theories and models inspire people to see the workplace
   through new lenses. A major one is the learning organization, developed by
   Peter Senge in *The Fifth Discipline: The Art and Practice of the Learning
   Organization* (Doubleday Business, 1994). The first four disciplines are
   personal mastery, mental models, shared visions, and team learning. The
   fifth discipline, systems thinking, integrates the other four.
      Other concepts include the agile mindset, which started as a software
   development method and is now also used as a management model.
      Intrapreneurship, still another, is based on behaving like entrepreneurs
   while working inside an organization by taking direct responsibility for
   turning an idea into a profitable finished product.
      Another one experimented with by a few organizations is the liberated
   company. Few companies have gone all the way with this model, as it is based
   on giving employees complete freedom and responsibility to take the actions
   they deem best.

The Teal organization, a paradigm created by Frederic Laloux and explored in *Reinventing Organizations* (Nelson Parker, 2014), is based on self-steering, lack of hierarchy, and little control in terms of rules and mechanisms.

There is an excellent list with references in the BCG article "The End of Bureaucracy, Again?" by Martin Reeves, Edzard Wesselink, and Kevin Whitaker (BCG Henderson Institute, July 27, 2020). Accessed August 24, 2020, at www.bcg.com/en-us/publications/2020/changing-business-environment-pushing-end-to-bureaucracy.

These theories and models, along with others not listed here, are all part of the slow movement, started over 50 years ago, away from the traditional mindset and toward the gig mindset, though the term is not used. The "Pioneers of the Gig Mindset Inside Organizations" section in "Recommended Reading" offers a nonexhaustive list of key works since 1960.

**PART 2: THE FUTURE IS AT STAKE**

1   *Self-Efficacy: The Exercise of Control*, Albert Bandura (W.H. Freeman, 1997). You can also study Bandura's work in his book *Social Learning Theory* (Prentice-Hall: 1st ed., 1976). The Wikipedia page about the book offers a detailed summary and additional information, accessed July 27, 2020, at en.wikipedia.org/wiki/Self-Efficacy_(book).

For an overview of the concept of social learning, I recommend reading the Wikipedia page at en.wikipedia.org/wiki/Social_learning_theory, accessed July 27, 2020. The historical overview starts with B.F. Skinner's behaviorist theories, goes through the work of several professors and psychologists, taking us to the context in which Bandura and others further developed the concept and applied it to various fields.

2   The World Economic Forum, self-described on its website as an international organization for public-private cooperation; "The Forum engages the foremost political, business, cultural and other leaders of society to shape global, regional and industry agendas. It was established in 1971 as a not-for-profit foundation and is headquartered in Geneva, Switzerland." Accessed August 2, 2020, at www.weforum.org/about/world-economic-forum.

Data for the 2018 World Economic Forum (WEF) report come from a set of companies that represent 15 million workers. The report is downloadable from the WEF website at www.weforum.org/reports/the-future-of-jobs-report-2018, accessed July 27, 2020. The 2016 report is available at www3.weforum.org/docs/WEF_Future_of_Jobs.pdf, accessed July 27, 2020.

The Occupational Information Network (O*NET) framework was used by the authors of the WEF reports for its categories of analysis for jobs, skills, and tasks. The O*NET Database is sponsored by the US Department of Labor, Employment and Training Administration (USDOL/ETA) and developed by the National Center for O*NET Development. The database content is published under a Creative Commons Attribution 4.0 International license.

More information here: www.onetcenter.org/license_db.html, accessed July 27, 2020.

3   Willful blindness is a concept developed by Margaret Heffernan in her bestselling book *Willful Blindness: Why We Ignore the Obvious at Our Peril* (Bloomsbury USA, 2011). The concept originated in the field of law and refers to situations where people are responsible for things they should have or could have known but instead claimed they did not. Heffernan's book offers examples from many domains. In this book I use the term to describe the attitude of many senior managers who are unconsciously or deliberately unaware of change internally and externally, and how this results in negative reactions to the gig mindset.

4   www.netjmc.com/the-hr-edge-joker-card-in-the-intranet-game/.

5   www.netjmc.com/hr-stuck-in-the-middle-management-versus-people/.

6   C.K. Prahalad, "Why Is It So Hard to Tackle the Obvious?" a June 2010 *Harvard Business Review* column, accessed July 27, 2020, at hbr.org/2010/06/column-why-is-it-so-hard-to-tackle-the-obvious. Prahalad (1941–2010) was a well-known corporate strategist.

A related article, "Best Practices Get You Only So Far," published in April 2010 in *Harvard Business Review* and also by Prahalad, continues in the same vein. Accessed July 27, 2020, at hbr.org/2010/04/column-best-practices-get-you-only-so-far.

The forgetting curve and learning curve referred to in Prahalad's "Why Is It So Hard to Tackle the Obvious?" were defined by the German psychologist Hermann Ebbinghaus, a pioneer in the study of memory, who lived from 1850 to 1909. Wikipedia provides a detailed overview of his work at en.wikipedia.org/wiki/Hermann_Ebbinghaus, accessed August 1, 2020.

7   Read about the how Astalift started at www.astalift.com.sg/about-astalift/, accessed July 27, 2020.

8   Survey participants placed themselves on a 5-point scale, with 1 being a highly traditional mindset and 5 a highly gig mindset. They were divided into two groups: lower gig mindset, if their average score was under 4.0, and higher gig mindset if it was 4.0 or above. There were 127 people in the first group and 169 in the second. This analysis helped us understand differences in degree within the gig mindset, as it was based on people who had volunteered to take part in a survey specifically about the gig mindset. It should not be interpreted as indicative of the breakdown between gig and traditional mindsets within an organization or in the working population in general.

9   An October 29, 2018, article in the *Financial Times* by Andrew Jack compares the case-study emphasis at Harvard University and the scenario emphasis at Yale University. "Why Harvard's Case Studies Are Under Fire," accessed July 27, 2020, at www.ft.com/content/0b1aeb22-d765-11e8-a854-33d6f82e62f8.

10  The concept of positive deviance originated in the field of nutrition and has been adopted by and adapted to other contexts, including organizational behavior.

These links, accessed July 27, 2020, provide information from different perspectives:

positivedeviance.org

en.wikipedia.org/wiki/Positive_deviance

www.bus.umich.edu/FacultyResearch/Research/research-8-04 understanding_040704.htm

positivedeviance.org/the-power-of-positive-deviance

11 Brian Walker and David Salt, *Resilience Thinking: Sustaining Ecosystems and People in a Changing World* (Island Press, 2006).

### PART 3: BUILDING PROACTIVE RESILIENCE

1 BSI *Organizational Resilience Index Report 2017*, p. 11. More information, including reports on organizational resilience, can be found on the British Standards Institution website at www.bsigroup.com/, accessed July 27, 2020.

2 D. Christopher Kayes, professor of management at the George Washington University School of Business in Washington, DC, is quoted extensively in the Economist Intelligence Unit's report *Organisational Resilience: Building an Enduring Enterprise*. The report, commissioned by the British Standards Institution, was published in December 2015. It can be viewed at this link, accessed July 27, 2020: www.slideshare.net/BSIGroupThailand/organizational-resiliencecranfieldresearchreport.

3 "The Quest for Resilience," by Gary Hamel and Liisa Välikangas, in *Harvard Business Review*, September 2003, accessed July 25, 2020, hbr. org/2003/09/the-quest-for-resilience.

4 The BSI reports can be found on its website, www.bsigroup.com/.

Here is the link to the 2019 report, accessed July 27, 2020: www.bsigroup. com/LocalFiles/pt-BR/organizational-resilience/or-index-2019-web-final.pdf. All 16 elements are presented and compared. Over a thousand organizations were surveyed.

5 There are numerous explanations of what happened to Nokia. Here are two I found interesting, both accessed July 25, 2020, at the links below:

"Where Nokia Went Wrong," by James Surowiecki, author of *The Wisdom of Crowds*, www.newyorker.com/business/currency/where-nokia-went-wrong.

"The Strategic Decisions That Caused Nokia's Failure," by Yves L. Doz, emeritus professor of Strategic Management at INSEAD. knowledge.insead. edu/strategy/the-strategic-decisions-that-caused-nokias-failure-7766.

6 I originally published this list on the Global Peter Drucker Forum blog in July 2017. Accessed July 26, 2020, at www.druckerforum.org/blog/?p=1536.

### PART 4: OPENING MINDS AND ORGANIZATIONS

1 wirearchy.com/what-is-wirearchy/.

2 The Foundational Framework used in my research on the organization in the digital age has nine components, one of which is leadership. www.netjmc. com/foundational-framework/.

3 Weick is referring to the concept of a "spirit of contradiction" used by Eric-Hans Kramer in his work about dynamic complexity, *Organizing Doubt: Grounded Theory, Army Units and Dealing with Dynamic Complexity* (Copenhagen Business School Press, 2007).

4 *Managing the Unexpected: Sustained Performance in a Complex World*, 3rd ed., by Karl E. Weick and Kathleen M. Sutcliffe (Jossey-Bass, 2015).

5 Gallup has done regular polls on the state of the global workplace that shook up the corporate world because of the shockingly low level of employee engagement. You can find details on its website. This link, accessed August 2, 2020, will get you started: www.gallup.com/workplace/257552/state-global-workplace-2017.aspx.

6 My October 13, 2017, article in the MIT *Sloan Management Review* is about how to neutralize internal politics in digital initiatives. Defining fundamental principles was an important part of the approach. Accessed August 27, 2020, at sloanreview.mit.edu/article/neutralize-internal-politics-in-digital-initiatives/.

7 *Making Sense of the Organization*, vol. 2: *The Impermanent Organization*, by Karl E. Weick (John Wiley & Sons, 2009).

8 I wrote about company cultures that help (or hinder) digital transformation and the importance of getting input directly from the people at the edges of the organization in this article, published August 28, 2015, in the *Harvard Business Review*. Accessed August 27, 2020, at hbr.org/2015/08/the-company-cultures-that-help-or-hinder-digital-transformation.

I wrote about a related theme: how leaders inspire engagement by sharing decision-making with people on the edges, often customer-facing, in an April 27, 2018, article in MIT *Sloan Management Review*. Accessed August 27, 2020, at sloanreview.mit.edu/article/how-digital-leaders-inspire-engagement/.

9 *Making Sense of the Organization*, vol. 2: *The Impermanent Organization*, by Karl E. Weick (John Wiley & Sons, 2009, Kindle edition, pp. 264–65).

10 "The Ten Principles of Digital Work," by Esko Kilpi, May 31, 2018. Accessed August 2, 2020, at medium.com/@EskoKilpi/the-ten-principles-of-digital-work-67a2f3462000.

Esko died in early 2020, leaving us with a wealth of wisdom he shared on Twitter, Medium, and his website, Interactive Value Creation, accessed August 2, 2020, at www.kilpi.fi. I suggest you explore the articles and materials via his website.

11 Work Is Learning & Learning Is the Work, the website of Harold Jarche, where he develops his work about personal knowledge mastery. Accessed August 2, 2020, at jarche.com. His posts are insightful and thought-provoking, and merit reading.

12 I described a short conversation I had with Esko Kilpi on Twitter in this blog post: "Does Knowledge Walk When People Walk?" www.netjmc.com/does-knowledge-walk-when-people-walk/.

13 These figures are from my annual research surveys and reports about organizations in the digital age, available at www.netjmc.com/a-decade-of-research/.

14 "How to Scale Up Learning," Esko Kilpi, February 18, 2019, accessed August 2, 2020, at medium.com/@EskoKilpi/how-to-scale-up-learning-997fcbc12827.

15 Bryce Williams coined the term "work out loud." See thebryceswrite.com/2010/11/29/when-will-we-work-out-loud-soon/.

16 I wrote about it in "Working Out Loud Is Natural for Gig Mindsetters," at www.netjmc.com/working-out-loud-is-natural-for-gig-mindsetters/.

17 From Roger Launius, "Comments on a Very Effective Communications System: Marshall Space Flight Center's Monday Notes," February 28, 2011, accessed August 28, 2020, launiusr.wordpress.com/2011/02/28/comments-on-a-very-effective-communications-system-marshall-space-flight-center's-monday-notes/.

18 Take a look at my original article, "Working Out Loud from the Top—Half a Century Ago at NASA," at www.netjmc.com/working-out-loud-from-the-top-half-a-century-ago-at-nasa/.

19 Interesting articles to read about accidental discoveries:

www.sciencealert.com/these-eighteen-accidental-scientific-discoveries-changed-the-world.

www.popularmechanics.com/science/health/g1216/10-awesome-accidental-discoveries/.

www.rd.com/funny-stuff/10-accidental-discoveries-put-to-good-use/.

20 The concept of sets of control is part of the minimal structure concept summarized by Miguel Pina e Cunha, João Vieira da Cunha, and Ken Kamoche in their 2003 article "Organizational Improvisation: What, When, How and Why," *International Journal of Management Reviews*, vol. 1, no. 3, pp. 299–341. In the article, they refer to work and writings by many researchers, too numerous to mention here.

21 "Swift Trust and Temporary Groups," by Debra Meyerson, Karl E. Weick, and Roderick M. Kramer, chapter 9 in *Trust in Organizations: Frontiers of Theory and Research* by Roderick M. Kramer and Tom R. Tyler (SAGE, 1996, pp. 166–95).

For an interesting history of swift trust, see Wikipedia at en.wikipedia.org/wiki/Swift_trust_theory#Swift_trust_in_different_work_teams, accessed July 27, 2020.

22 The authors of the paper are Allègre L. Hadida, William Tarvainen, and Jed Rose. First published September 15, 2014, in *International Journal of Management Reviews* and available in free access at doi.org/10.1111/ijmr.12047, accessed August 22, 2020.

23 Checklist designed from data in "Culture and Organizational Improvisation in UK Financial Services," a study done by Stephen A. Leybourne, Boston University. *Journal of Service Science and Management*, vol. 2, no. 4 (2009), pp. 237–54. doi: 10.4236/jssm.2009.24029.

There is a wealth of additional material on Stephen Leybourne's personal and research web pages at Boston University, blogs.bu.edu/sleyb/publications/.

24 Email conversation with Stephen A. Leybourne on May 22, 2020, reprinted with permission.

25 Read about the pizza guy in the April 10, 2020, BBC article "Coronavirus: I'm Using My Pizza Oven to Toss Masks for Nurses," accessed April 15, 2020, at www.bbc.com/news/world-us-canada-52232381.

26 "Emergency 'Skuba' Mask Validated for Healthcare Use," April 8, 2020, accessed April 15, 2020, at www.news-medical.net/news/20200408/Emergency-Skuba-mask-validated-for-healthcare-use.aspx.

27 "French Sports Retailer Gives Diving Masks to Caregivers," April 4, 2020, accessed April 15, 2020, at www.aa.Com.tr/en/europe/french-sports-retailer-gives-diving-masks-to-caregivers/1792150.

28 "Burn-out an 'Occupational Phenomenon': International Classification of Diseases," WHO, May 28, 2019, accessed October 2, 2020, at www.who.int/mental_health/evidence/burn-out/en/.

It is being recognized now that burnout is usually caused by organizations and is not a sign that individual people are weak. If you want to explore the topic more, this NPR article is a good starting point: www.npr.org/sections/health-shots/2019/05/28/727637944/who-redefines-burnout-as-a-syndrome-linked-to-chronic-stress-at-work, accessed October 2, 2020.

29 Research has been done on burnout, and specifically a study by Linda V. Heinemann and Torsten Heinemann that looked at all the research carried out in the 40-year period leading up to 2011. "Burnout Research: Emergence and Scientific Investigation of a Contested Diagnosis" (March 6, 2017) has been published in open access mode on SAGE Open: journals.sagepub.com/doi/10.1177/2158244017697154, accessed October 2, 2020.

30 "Employee Burnout Is a Problem with the Company, Not the Person," by Eric Garton, *Harvard Business Review*, April 6, 2017. Accessed July 25, 2020, at hbr.org/2017/04/employee-burnout-is-a-problem-with-the-company-not-the-person. Garton's article is short and well worth reading for the practical advice he offers. Garton is coauthor, with Michael Mankins, of *Time, Talent, Energy: Overcome Organizational Drag and Unleash Your Team's Productive Power* (HBR Press, 2017).

31 "Job Burnout: How to Spot It and Take Action," accessed July 26, 2020, at www.mayoclinic.org/healthy-lifestyle/adult-health/in-depth/burnout/art-20046642.

32 The relationship between work conditions and long-term health has been studied by researchers. Jared Lindzon wrote an article published in *Fast Company*, reporting on the research conducted by Erik Gonzalez-Mulé and Bethany Cockburn from Indiana University's Kelley School of Business about the relationship between long-term health and work conditions such as stress and personal control. The research included a seven-year longitudinal study; the hypothesis was then tested using data from the similar Wisconsin

Longitudinal Study. The *Fast Company* article summarizes the results. "Study Finds Work-Life Balance Could Be a Matter of Life and Death," October 20, 2016. Accessed July 26, 2020, at www.fastcompany.com/3064755/study-finds-work-life-balance-could-be-a-matter-of-life-and-death.
The original research results were first presented at the 2015 Academy of Management Conference in Vancouver, then published September 2, 2016, in "Worked to Death: The Relationships of Job Demands and Job Control with Mortality," *Journal of Personnel Psychology*. Available at the Wiley Online Library for subscribers or access via several short-access paid options. Accessed July 25, 2020, at onlinelibrary.wiley.com/doi/abs/10.1111/peps.12206.

**PART 5: INVESTING IN THE MOVERS**
1  BSI *Organizational Resilience Index Report 2019*, accessed July 25, 2020, at www.bsigroup.com/en-GB/our-services/Organizational-Resilience/Organizational-Resilience-Index/.
2  The definitions are from *Cambridge Dictionary* and *Merriam-Webster* online; dictionary.cambridge.org/dictionary/english/job and www.merriam-webster.com/dictionary/job, both accessed July 25, 2020.
3  www.businessdictionary.com/definition/job.html, accessed October 8, 2020.
4  Jon Husband's website, accessed August 27, 2020, at wirearchy.com.
5  Accessed August 2, 2020, at www.gallup.com/workplace/257552/state-global-workplace-2017.aspx.
6  Accessed July 25, 2020, at www.urbandictionary.com/define.php?term=job.
7  Interview with Subramanian S. Kalpathi, India, author of *The Millennials: Exploring the World of the Largest Living Generation* (Random Business, 2016). Kalpathi was a speaker at Davos in 2016.
8  Conversation with Harold Jarche, whose website has many relevant articles. www.jarche.com, accessed August 27, 2020.
9  Little has been published about the concept, originally defined in "Building the Velcro Organization: Creating Value through Integration and Maintaining Organization-Wide Efficiency," by Joseph L. Bower, the Donald K. David Professor of Business Administration at the Harvard Business School and author of 12 books. The article was published in the November–December 2003 issue of *Ivey Business Journal*.
10  Ronald A. Heifetz and Donald L. Laurie have written extensively about adaptive challenges, including in the article "The Work of Leadership," in the *Harvard Business Review*, December 2001, at hbr.org/2001/12/the-work-of-leadership. Heifetz also wrote, with coauthor Marty Linsky, *Leadership on the Line* (Harvard Business School Press, 2002).
11  Chris Catliff, "Three Ways to Fire Up Employee Passion," *Globe and Mail*, April 3, 2018, www.theglobeandmail.com/business/careers/leadership/article-three-ways-to-fire-up-employee-passion/.

PART 6: DEFINING A PERPETUAL BALANCE

1   *Polarity Management: Identifying and Managing Unsolvable Problems*, by Barry Johnson (HRD Press, Kindle edition, 1996).

PART 7: OWNING YOUR PERSONAL STRATEGY

1   Read more about transformational leadership on Wikipedia in a long but interesting article with many examples at en.wikipedia.org/wiki/Transformational_leadership, accessed August 5, 2020.

2   *The Age of Unreason*, by Charles Handy. First published in 1989 in paperback in Great Britain by Business Books, then in the US in 1990 by Harvard Business School Press in hardback. Handy discusses the shamrock organization in detail, with lots of examples and provocative commentary, in chapter 4, "The Shamrock Organization" (p. 962, location 962 of 3059 in the Kindle edition of the book, Cornerstone Digital; new ed., 2012).

3   CareerCast, producer of the *Jobs Rated Report*, a job-ranking service based on certain criteria, including income level, reported that mathematician jumped up 17 places from the previous year's ranking of jobs and is expected to grow by 23 percent by 2022. Accessed August 5, 2020, at www.careercast.com/jobs-rated/2019-jobs-rated-report.

4   www.aligunjan.com/Imaginarium-Aligunjan.pdf, p. 5, accessed October 3, 2020.

APPENDIX B: EVOLUTION OF THE WORKPLACE

1   "Tracking the Trends in Bringing Our Own Devices to Work," authored by me and published in *Harvard Business Review* on May 4, 2016. Accessed August 27, 2020, at hbr.org/2016/05/tracking-the-trends-in-bringing-our-own-devices-to-work.

RECOMMENDED READING

1   Britannica.com/topic/Web-20 and Arstechnica.com/information-technology/2006/09/7650/, both accessed October 8, 2020.

# Index

5, *38*, *51*, 52, 76, 80–83, *134*, *137*, *190*, 214, 226n15
fear: of losing power, 31–32; overcoming fear, 158–59; of speed, 32–34, *33*
flexibility, 214. *See also* resilience, proactive
forgetting curve, 30, 223n6
Foundational Framework for the Organization in the Digital Age, 209–11, *210*, 212, *212*
framework, freedom within, 68–72
freelancing, 160–61
Fujifilm, 31
fundamental principles, 69–72, 225n6
future, focus on, 30, 42–43
*The Future of Jobs Report* (World Economic Forum), 26–27, 222n2

Gallup, 111, 225n5
Garton, Eric, 96
gig mindset and gig mindsetters: about and approach to, 1, *2*, 8–9, 10–11, 12–13, 16, 175–76, 182; author's gradual awareness of, xiii–xv; as border crossers, 21–22; as bottom-up movement, 7–8; boundary pushing by, 178–80; career growth and, 6, 120–21; case study lessons, 176–78; characteristics and traits, 20–27, 189, *190–91*; as civil disobedience, 15–16, 20; common reactions to, 6–7; vs. dependence on best practices and benchmarking, 30–31; as detectors, 23–24; vs. false sense of security in silos, 34–35; vs. fear of losing power, 31–32; vs. fear of speed, 32–34, *33*; functions and job roles suited for, *196*, 197; generational gap, 151; hiring practices and recruitment, 108–9, 112–15, *113*, 141–42; importance of, 3, 150; as influencers, 25–26; as inside outsiders, 22–23; vs. living in filter bubbles, 35–37; myths about, 107–8; as new identity, xvi–xvii; performance

evaluations, 115–20; as positive deviance, 38, *38–39*; vs. pride in past success, 28–30; questions to ask, 3–4, 198; reader profiles and, 11–12; research (survey) on, xv, xv–xvi, 17, 199–202, 221nn1–2, 223n8; resilience and, 54–55, *54–55*; rethinking jobs, 109–12; role within organizations, 1–3; in shamrock organizations, 162–65; soft skills and, 26–27; starting points, 180–82; technological capabilities underlying, 17, *18*, 207–8; vs. traditional mindset, 5–6, 18, *19*, 179–80; upsides and downsides, 133, 139–40, *140*, 191, *193*, *195*. *See also* openers; personal strategies, for gig mindset
gig mindset–traditional mindset spectrum, 131–48; about, 10–11, 131–32; ACTC case study, 145–48, 177, 204; decision-making framework for, 133, 142–45, *143*, *144*; finding balance, overview, 132–33; identifying group's position on, 133, 136, *136–38*, 139; identifying personal position on, 132, 133, *134–35*, 135, *157*, 157–58; identifying upsides and downsides of each mindset, 133, 139–40, *140*, 191, *192–95*; polarities and, 132, 156–57; recruitment considerations during transition, 141–42
goals, 177, 180, 200; job, 111
Gonzalez-Mulé, Erik, 101, 227n32
Google, 30
group, vs. individual, 178
Gupta, Indrajit, 27, 66–67

Hamel, Gary, 46–47
Handy, Charles, 162. *See also* shamrock organizations
health, and work conditions, 100, 227n32. *See also* burnout
Heffernan, Margaret, 223n3
Heinemann, Linda V., 95, 227n29
Heinemann, Torsten, 95, 227n29
hierarchy speak, 110